PENGUIN BOOKS — GREAT IDEAS

What is Existentialism?

T0018186

Simone de Beauvoir

1908–1986

Simone de Beauvoir

What is Existentialism?

Translated by Marybeth Timmermann

PENGUIN BOOKS — GREAT IDEAS

PENGUIN BOOKS

UK | USA | Canada | Ireland | Australia
India | New Zealand | South Africa

Penguin Books is part of the Penguin Random House group
of companies whose addresses can be found at
global.penguinrandomhouse.com.

Penguin
Random House
UK

'What is Existentialism?' first published as 'Qu'est-ce que
l'existentialisme?' in *France-Amériques* no, 59 (June 29, 1947).
Translation first published in *Philosophical Writings*. Copyright 2005
Board of Trustees of the University of Illinois. Used with permission
of the University of Illinois Press.

Text copyright © Sylvie Le Bon de Beauvoir
Translation copyright © Marybeth Timmermann, 2004

'Pyrrhus and Cineas' first published as *Pyrrhus et Cineas*
(Gallimard, 1944). Translation first published in *Philosophical Writings*.
Copyright 2005 Board of Trustees of the University of Illinois.
Used with permission of the University of Illinois Press.

Text copyright © Éditions Gallimard, 1944
Translation copyright © Marybeth Timmermann, 2004

This selection published in Penguin Books 2020

007

Set in 12/15 pt Dante MT Std
Typeset by Jouve (UK), Milton Keynes
Printed and bound in Great Britain by Clays Ltd, Elcograf S.p.A.

A CIP catalogue record for this book
is available from the British Library

ISBN: 978-0-241-47523-2

www.greenpenguin.co.uk

MIX
Paper from
responsible sources
FSC® C018179
www.fsc.org

Penguin Random House is committed to a
sustainable future for our business, our readers
and our planet. This book is made from Forest
Stewardship Council® certified paper.

Contents

What is Existentialism?

I don't know how many times during my trip to America someone made this request, which was also familiar to me in France: 'Can you explain what existentialism is?' And my interlocutor, undoubtedly curious about any novelty yet sparing with his time and effort, would add, 'in a few words' or 'in five minutes.' I disappointed many amiable people and made several journalists unhappy by refusing to comply. Some doubted my intellectual capacities; others were suspicious of a doctrine that could not be summarized in one sentence. However, at the risk of disappointing once again, I must say right away that even an article is not enough to give an account of existentialism. I only intend to dissipate some misunderstandings here.

The first error consists precisely in believing that existentialism can be concentrated in one or two immediately efficient, simple expressions. It is not a martingale that guarantees winning at the game of life, nor a recipe capable of erasing the annoyances of existence. Neither is it the art of interpreting dreams, evoking spirits, or holding seances. One must not expect any of these distractions that are so agreeable in society. It is not a social phenomenon analogous to the zazou phenomenon, nor a political movement, nor a postwar fashion, even though it has social repercussions, it does include political implications, and fashion has both served and dis-served it. Even less is it a predilection for scandal; the Parisian public who rushed to the first existentialist conferences in the hopes of seeing surrealist extrava-gances again were extremely disappointed to have to listen to a serious doctrinal lecture like a class at the Sorbonne. Existentialism is first of all a phil-osophy, analogous in many aspects to classical philosophies and discussed in places as austere and respectable as the French Society of Philosophy [La société française de philosophie], for example.

No one would dream of demanding that the system of Kant or Hegel be dispensed in three sentences; existentialism does not lend itself to pop-ularization any easier. A philosophical theory, like a physics or mathematical theory, is accessible only to the initiated. Indeed, it is indispensable to be famil-iar with the long tradition upon which it rests if one wants to grasp both the foundations and the origin-ality of the new doctrine. How could you show the audacity of Einstein or de Broglie to someone who was unaware of Newton's mechanics?

The problem is the same here. Many criticisms addressed to us by uninformed minds are aimed at Descartes or Kant rather than existentialism. It is very often philosophy in general that is being questioned by attacking us. In truth, several years of study are needed to be able to detect existentialism's original contribution to philosophy and to be in a position to discuss the validity of it.

However, the fact that non-specialists, regardless of their incompetence, are interested in existentialism must have an explanation. Symbolic logic, for example, never incited such passionate disputes. The reason, in fact, is that although existentialism claims to rest upon the most serious theoretical bases, it also claims to be a practical and living attitude toward the problems posed by the world today. It is a philosophy yet does not want to stay enclosed in books and schools; it intends to revive the great tradition of ancient wisdom that also involved difficult physics and logic, yet proposed a concrete human attitude to all men. This is why it is not expressed solely in theoretical and abstract treatises but also strives to reach a larger public through novels and plays. This attempt disconcerts many people and makes them doubt that existentialism is truly a philosophy. But this is misunderstanding the truth of philosophy, which, particularly in France, has never appeared as a singular discipline but as a global vision of the world and of man that must embrace the totality of the human domain. Today, the ideologies that gain the approval of most French intellectuals, namely Christianity, existentialism, and Marxism, all have a common pretension of showing man in entirety. They all respond to the same need: in France and all across Europe the individual is seeking with anguish to find his place in a world turned upside down.

Pascal summarized the ambiguity of the relationship between the Universe and man in a famous and striking expression when he called man a thinking reed. From this definition, Christianity retains essentially the aspect of interiority: in the secret of his heart, by the purity of his intentions, and by the individual accomplishment of the ethics dictated by his conscience, man will attain his salvation in this world. On the contrary, Marxism emphasizes that man is a reed, a thing among things, definable by his relationship with the objective reality of the world.

Existentialism strives to hold both ends of the chain at the same time, surpassing [*dépassant*] the interior-exterior, subjective-objective opposition. It postulates the value of the individual as the source and reason for being [*raison d'être*] of all significations and all colours, yet it admits that the individual has reality only through his engagement in the world. It affirms that the will of free being is sufficient for the accomplishment of freedom, yet it also states that this will can posit itself only by struggling against the obstacles and the oppressions that limit the concrete possibilities of man. It resembles individualism in the sense that it seems important to it that each individual gains his own salvation, and that each individual appears as being the only one able to obtain it for himself. Yet it also resembles Marxist realism because only in working actively for the concrete triumph of universal freedom, by proposing ends for himself that surpass him, can the individual hope to save himself. Thereby existentialism also seeks a reconciliation of those two reigns whose divorce is so nefarious to men in our time: the ethical reign and the political reign. Ethics appears to existentialism not as the formal respect of eternal and supraterrestrial laws, but as the search for a valid foundation of human history, such as it unfolds on our earth. Politics is not, for existentialism, the simple adjustment of the efficient means toward an unconditioned end, but the perpetual and incessant creation and construction of the end by the means used to produce it. In other words, the task of man is one: to fashion the world by giving it a meaning. This meaning is not given ahead of time, just as the existence of each man is not justified ahead of time either.

Along with the idea of a God guaranteeing Good and Evil, existentialism rejects the notion of ready-made values whose affirmation precedes human judgment. By freely taking his own freedom as an end within himself and in his acts, man constitutes a kingdom of ends. Cut off from human will, the reality of the world is but an 'absurd given'. This is a conception that appears to many people as hopeless and makes them accuse existentialism of being pessimistic. But actually there is no hopelessness, since we think that it is possible for man to snatch the world from the darkness of absurdity, clothe it in significations, and project valid goals into it. We very simply rediscover the wisdom of old Montaigne, who said, 'Life is in itself neither good nor evil; it is the place of good or evil as you make them!' The fact is that the old labels, idealism-realism, individualism-universalism, pessimism-optimism, cannot be applied to a doctrine that is precisely an effort to surpass these oppositions in a new synthesis, respecting the fundamental ambiguity of the world, of man, and of their relationship.

Such a novelty, I repeat, can hardly be summarized; it reveals itself only by a direct intuition that must be sought in the works where it is presented, and that bears fruit only if one takes the time to let it ripen within oneself.

Pyrrhus and Cineas

Plutarch tells us that one day Pyrrhus was devising projects of conquest. 'We are going to subjugate Greece first,' he was saying. 'And after that?' said Cineas. 'We will vanquish Africa.' – 'After Africa?' – 'We will go on to Asia, we will conquer Asia Minor, Arabia.' – 'And after that?' – 'We will go on as far as India.' – 'After India?' – 'Ah!' said Pyrrhus, 'I will rest.' – 'Why not rest right away?' said Cineas.

Cineas seems wise. What's the use of leaving if it is to return home? What's the use of starting if you must stop? And yet, if I don't first decide to stop, it seems to me to be even more pointless to leave. 'I will not say A,' says the schoolboy stubbornly. 'But why?' – 'Because, after that, I will have to say B.' He knows that if he starts, he will never be finished with it: after B, it will be the entire alphabet, syllables, words, books, tests, and a career. Each minute a new task will throw him forward toward a new task, without rest. If it is never to be finished, what's the use of starting? Even the architect of the Tower of Babel thought that the sky was a ceiling and that someone would reach it one day. If Pyrrhus could push the limits of his conquests back beyond the earth, beyond the stars and the furthest nebulae, to an infinity that would be constantly fleeing before him, his undertaking would only be more foolish because of it. His efforts would be dispersed without ever coming together for any goal. Viewed by reflection, all human projects therefore seem absurd because they exist only by setting limits for themselves, and one can always overstep these limits, asking oneself derisively, 'Why as far as this? Why not further? What's the use?'

'I found that no goal was worth the trouble of any effort,' said Benjamin Constant's hero. Such are often the thoughts of the adolescent when the voice of reflection awakens in him. As a child, he was like Pyrrhus: he ran, he played without asking himself questions, and the objects that he created seemed to him endowed with an absolute existence. They carried within themselves their reason for being. But he discovered one day that he had the power to surpass [dépasser] his own ends. There are no longer ends; only pointless occupations still exist for him; he rejects them. 'The dice are loaded,' he says. He looks at his elders with scorn: how is it possible for them to believe in their undertakings? They are dupes. Some have killed themselves in order to put an end to this ridiculous illusion. And it was indeed the only way to end it, because as long as I remain alive, Cineas harasses me in vain, saying: 'And after that? What's the use?' In spite of everything, my heart beats, my hand reaches out, new projects are born and push me forward. Wise men have wanted to see the sign of man's incurable folly in this stubbornness. But can a perversion so essential still be called perversion? Where will we find the truth about man if it is not in him? Reflection cannot stop the élan of our spontaneity.

But reflection is also spontaneous. Man plants, builds, conquers; he wants, he loves: there is always an 'after that?' It could be that from moment to moment he throws himself into new undertakings with an ardour that is always new, like Don Juan deserting one woman only to seduce another. But even Don Juan gets tired one fine day.

Between Pyrrhus and Cineas the dialogue starts over with no end.

And yet, Pyrrhus must decide. He stays or he leaves. If he stays, what will he do? If he leaves, how far will he go?

'We must cultivate our garden,' says Candide. This advice will not be of much help to us because what is my garden? There are men who claim to work the entire earth, and others will find a pot of flowers too vast. Some say carelessly, 'What happens when we're gone is none of our concern,' while the dying Charlemagne cried at the sight of the Normans' ships. A young woman gets irritated because she has leaky shoes that take in water. If I say to her: 'What does that matter? Think of the millions of men who are dying of hunger in the middle of China,' she answers me angrily: 'They are in China. And it's my shoe that has a hole.' However, another woman may cry about the horror of the Chinese famine. If I say to her: 'What does that matter to you? You are not hungry,' she would look at me with scorn: 'What does my own comfort matter?' So how to know what is mine? The disciples of Christ asked: who is my neighbour?

What, then, is the measure of a man? What goals can he set for himself, and what hopes are permitted him?

PART I

Candide's Garden

I knew a child who cried because his concierge's son had died. His parents let him cry, and then they got annoyed. 'After all, that little boy was not your brother.' The child dried his tears. But that was a dangerous thing to teach. Useless to cry over a little boy who is a stranger: so be it. But why cry over one's brother? 'It's none of your business,' says the woman holding back her husband who wants to join in a fight. The husband goes away, docile. But if the woman asks for his help a few minutes later, saying: 'I'm tired, I'm cold,' he looks at her with surprise from the heart of the solitude where he has withdrawn, thinking: 'Is that *my* business?' What does India matter? And what does Epirus matter? Why call this soil, this woman, these children *mine*? I brought these children into the world; they are here. The woman is next to me; the soil is under my feet. No tie exists between them and me. Mr Camus's Stranger thinks like this; he feels foreign to the whole world, which is completely foreign to him. Often during hardship man thus denies all his attachments. He does not want hardship; he looks for a way to flee from it. He looks within himself: he sees an indifferent body, a heart that beats to a steady rhythm. A voice says: 'I exist.' The hardship is not there. It is in the deserted house, on this dead face, in these streets. If I go within myself, I look at those inert streets with astonishment, saying: 'But what does it matter to me? All this is nothing to me.' I find myself indifferent, peaceful. 'But what has changed?' asked the sedentary petit bourgeois in September 1940, sitting in the midst of his belongings, 'We still eat the same steaks.' The changes only existed outside: what did they concern him?

If I myself were only a thing, nothing indeed would concern me. If I withdraw into myself, the other is also closed for me. The inert existence of things is separation and solitude. There exists no ready-made attachment between the world and me.

And as long as I am a simple given in the midst of nature, nothing is mine. A country is not mine if I only grew there like a plant. What is built up upon me, without me, is not mine. The rock that passively supports a house cannot claim that the house is its own. Mr Camus's Stranger is right to reject all those ties that others want to impose upon him from the outside; no tie is given at first. If a man is satisfied with a completely exterior relationship with the object, saying, 'My painting, my park, my workers' because a contract bestowed him with certain rights over these objects, it is because he is choosing to delude himself. He would like to spread out his place on earth, to expand his being beyond the limits of his body and his memory, yet without running the risk of any action. But the object facing him remains, indifferent, foreign. Social, organic, economic relationships are only external relationships and cannot be the foundation of any true possession.

In order to appropriate safely goods that are not our own, we can still resort to other ruses. Seated by his fire and reading in his newspaper the tale of someone who climbed the Himalayas, the contented bourgeois cries out proudly: 'Now there's what a man can do!' He feels like he climbed the Himalayas himself. By identifying himself with his sex, his country, his class, with the whole of humanity, a man can increase his garden, but he increases it only in words. This identification is but an empty pretension.

Only that in which I recognize my being is mine, and I can only recognize it where it is engaged. In order for an object to belong to me, it must have been founded by me. It is totally mine only if I founded it in its totality. The only reality that belongs entirely to me is, therefore, my act; even a work fashioned out of materials that are not mine escapes me in certain ways. What is mine is first the accomplishment of my project; a victory is mine if I fought for it. If the weary conqueror can rejoice in the victories of his son, it is because he wanted a son precisely in order to prolong his work; it is really the accomplishment of his own project that he salutes. It is because my subjectivity is not inertia, folding in upon itself, separation, but, on the contrary, movement toward the other that the difference between me and the other is abolished, and I can call the other mine. Only I can create the tie that unites me to the other. I create it from the fact that I am not a thing, but a project of self toward the other, a transcendence. And it is this power that Camus's Stranger is unaware of: no possession is given, but the foreign indifference of the world is not given either. I am not first a thing but a spontaneity that desires, that loves, that wants, that acts. 'That little boy *is* not my brother.' But if I cry over him, he is no longer a stranger to me. It's my tears that decide. Nothing is decided before me. When the disciples asked Christ: who is my neighbour? Christ didn't respond by an enumeration. He told the parable of the good Samaritan. The latter was the neighbour of the man abandoned on the road; he covered him with his cloak and came to his aid. One *is* not the neighbour of anyone; one makes the other a neighbour by making oneself [*se faisant*] his neighbour through an act.

What is mine is therefore first what I do. But as soon as I have done it, the object goes and separates itself from me; it escapes me. The thought that I expressed a moment ago, is it still my thought? In order for the past to be mine, I must make it mine again each instant by taking it toward my future. Even the objects that were not mine in the past because I didn't found them can be made into mine if I found something on them. I can rejoice in a victory in which I did not participate if I take it as a point of departure for my own conquests. The house that I did not build becomes my house if I live in it, and the earth my earth if I work it. My relationships with things are not given, are not fixed; I create them minute by minute. Some die, some are born, and others are revived. They are constantly changing. Each new act of surpassing [*dépassement*] gives me anew the thing surpassed, and that's why technologies are ways of appropriating the world: the sky belongs to those who know how to fly; the sea belongs to those who know how to swim and navigate.

Thus our relationship with the world is not decided from the onset; it is we who decide. But we do not arbitrarily decide just anything. What I surpass is always my past and the object such as it exists within that past. My future envelops that past; the former cannot build itself without the latter. The Chinese are my brothers from the moment I cry over their hardships, but one does not cry over the Chinese as he pleases. If I have never worried about Babylon, I cannot suddenly choose to be interested in the latest theories about the location of Babylon. I cannot suffer a defeat if I was not engaged in the vanquished country. I will suffer defeat in accordance with my engagements. A man who has fused his destiny with that of his country, its leader for example, could say '*my* defeat' in the face of the disaster. A man who has lived in a certain country without doing anything but eating and sleeping there will see the event only as a change of habits. It can happen that, in light of a new fact, one suddenly becomes aware of engagements that have been lived without being thought. But at least they had to have existed. As distinct from me, things never affect me; I am never affected except in my own possibilities.

We are therefore surrounded by forbidden wealth, and we often get irritated with these limits. We would like the entire world to become ours; we covet the goods of others. I knew, among others, one young student who wanted first to make the world of the athlete hers, then that of the gambler, the flirt, the adventurer, the politician, one after another. She tried her hand in each of these domains, without understanding that she remained a student hungry for experience. She believed that she was 'varying her life', but the unity of her life unified all of its diverse moments. An intellectual who takes the side of the proletariat does not become proletarian; he is an intellectual taking the side of the proletariat. The painting that Van Gogh paints is a new and free creation, but it is still a Van Gogh. If he claimed to paint a Gauguin, he would only make an imitation of Gauguin by Van Gogh. And that's why Candide's advice is superfluous: it's always *my* garden that I will cultivate. I am enclosed within it until death because that garden becomes mine from the moment I cultivate it.

In order for this piece of universe to belong to me,

however, I must truly cultivate it. Man's activity is often lazy. Instead of accomplishing true acts he contents himself with pretences: the fly on the stage-coach claims that he is the one who led the carriage to the top of the hill. To walk around talking about it, taking photographs of it, is not to participate in a war, in an expedition. There are even behaviours that contradict the ends that they claim to aim for: by establishing institutions that allow a sort of equilibrium in the midst of misery, the charitable lady tends to perpetuate the misery that she wants to alleviate. In order to know what is mine, I must know what I am really doing.

We see then that one can assign no dimension to the garden in which Candide wants to enclose me. It is not drawn out in advance; it is I who choose its location and limits.

And since, in any case, these limits are ridiculous compared to the infinity that surrounds me, wouldn't it be wise to reduce them as much as possible? The smaller it is, the less hold destiny will have over it. Let man therefore renounce all projects; let him imitate that judicious schoolboy who cried in order to not say A. Let him be like the god Indra, who, after having exhausted his strength in his victory over a fearsome demon, reduced himself to the dimensions of an atom and chose to live outside the world, under silent and indifferent waters, at the heart of a lotus stem.

The Instant

If I am no longer anything but a body, barely a place in the sun and the instant that measures my breath, then I am released from all worries, fears, as well as regrets. Nothing moves me, nothing matters to me. I attach myself only to this minute that my life is filling up, that alone is a tangible prey, a presence. Only the impression of the moment exists. There are empty moments that are only a sort of connecting fabric between the full moments; we patiently let them roll by. And in the instants of fullness, we will find ourselves satisfied, fulfilled. It's the moral of Aristippus, that of Horace's '*Carpe diem*', and Gide's *Nourritures terrestres* [The Fruits of the Earth]. Let us turn away from the world, from undertakings and conquests; let us devise no more projects; let us remain at home, at rest at the heart of our enjoyment.

But is enjoyment rest? Will we find it in us, and can it ever fulfill us?

'Enough, no more, 'Tis not so sweet now as it was before,' says the duke of Mantua to the musicians at the beginning of *Twelfth Night*. The sweetest melody, repeated indefinitely, becomes an annoying refrain. The taste at first delicious soon sickens me. An unchanging enjoyment that stays the same for too long is no longer felt as a plenitude; in the end it merges with a perfect absence. For enjoyment is the presence of an object to which I feel present. It is presence of the object and of myself in the heart of their difference. But as soon as the object is handed over to me, the difference dissolves. There is no longer an object, but once again a single, empty existence that is but vapidity and ennui. As soon as I eliminate the distance that, in separating me from the object, allows me to throw myself toward it, to be movement and transcendence, this fixed union of the object and me no longer exists except in the way a thing does. The Stoic can rightly put pleasure as well as pain among those realities that are foreign and indifferent to me since he defines them as a simple state that I can passively allow to continue within me.

But in reality, enjoyment is not a given fixed in the narrow envelope of the instant. Gide tells us that each pleasure envelops the entire world; the instant implies eternity; God is present in the sensation. Enjoyment is not a separation from the world; it assumes my existence in the world. And first of all it assumes the world's past, my past. A pleasure is even more precious if it is newer, if it stands out more intensely against the uniform background of time. But the instant limited to itself alone is not new; it is only new in its relationship with the past. That figure [*forme*] that just appeared is only distinct if the ground that supports it is itself distinct as ground. At the side of the sunny road the coolness of the shade is most precious, and a break is relaxing after tiring exercise. From the top of the hill I look at the path travelled, and the entire path is present in the joy of my success. The walk gives the rest its worth, and my thirst gives the glass of water its worth. A whole past comes together in the moment of enjoyment. And I don't just contemplate it. To enjoy a good thing is to use it, to throw oneself with it toward the future. To enjoy the sun or the shade is to feel its presence as a slow enrichment. I feel my strength being reborn in my relaxed body; I rest in order to leave again. While looking at the path travelled, I look at those valleys toward which I am going; I look at my future. All enjoyment is project. It surpasses the past toward the future, toward the world that is the fixed image of the future. To drink cinnamon-flavoured chocolate, says Gide in *Incidences*, is to drink Spain. Any perfume, any countryside that charms us throws us beyond itself, outside of ourselves. Reduced to itself, it would only be an inert and foreign existence. As soon as it falls back onto itself, enjoyment becomes ennui again. There is no enjoyment except when I leave myself and engage my being in the world through the object that I am enjoying. The psychasthèmes that Janet describes only experience a feeling of indifference before the most beautiful sights because no action forms within them. Flowers are no longer made to be plucked and smelled, paths no longer to be followed. The flowers seem made of painted metal; the countryside is no longer anything but a facade. There is no longer any future, no longer any surpassing, no longer any enjoyment. The world has lost all of its depth.

If man wants to rest in himself and tear himself away from the world, then he must renounce even enjoyment. The Epicureans knew this well; they scorned the pleasure of movement in order to preach only the pleasure of repose, pure ataraxia. And even better, the Stoics demanded that the wise man renounce even his body. Nothing is mine, they thought, but my pure interiority. I no longer have an exterior; I am but a naked presence that even pain cannot touch, an intangible upspringing [*jaillisse-ment*], gathered in the instant, and knowing only that it exists. So there is no longer good nor evil facing me, nor anxiety within me. I am, and nothing means anything to me anymore.

In this way the pouting child withdraws into a

corner and says: 'I don't care about anything.' But soon he looks around, he fidgets, he gets bored. When life withdraws into itself, it is not peaceful ataraxia but the anxiety of indifference that flees from itself, that tears itself away from itself, that appeals to the other. 'All the unhappiness of men arises from one single fact, that they cannot stay quietly in their own chamber,' says Pascal. But what if he cannot remain there? If he avoided all diversions, man would then find himself at the heart of what Valéry calls 'the pure ennui of living', and, as Valéry says, this purity 'instantly stops the heart.'

But is it then fitting to talk about 'diversions' and to say along with Valéry that it is 'reality in its pure state' that would be discovered at the heart of ennui? Hegel has shown convincingly that reality should never be conceived as an interiority hidden in the depths of appearance. Appearance hides nothing; it expresses. Interiority is not different from exteriority; appearance is itself reality. If man was only an atom of immobile presence, how would the illusion that the world is his and the appearance of desires and worries be born within him? If he is conscious of desiring and fearing, man desires and fears. If Pyrrhus's being was a being 'at rest', he wouldn't even be able to think about leaving. But he does think about it. As soon as he thinks about it, he has already left. 'Man is a being of faraway places,' says Heidegger; he is always *somewhere else*. There exists no privileged spot in the world about which he can safely say, 'This is me.' He is constitutively oriented toward something other than himself. He is himself only through relationships with something other than himself. 'Man is always infinitely more than he would be if he were reduced to what he is in the instant,' says Heidegger. Every thought, every look, every tendency is transcendence. This is what we have seen by considering enjoyment. It envelops the past, the future, the entire world. The man lying in the shade at the top of the hill is not only there, on that piece of earth that his body embraces. He is present to those hills that he perceives. He is also in the faraway cities, as someone who is absent. He rejoices in this absence. Even if he closes his eyes and tries to think about nothing, he feels like himself in contrast with the background of immobile and unconscious heat in which he bathes. He cannot suddenly spring forth into the world in the pure ipseity [selfness] of his being without the world suddenly springing forth in front of him.

It is because man is transcendence that it is so difficult for him ever to imagine any paradise. Paradise is rest; it is transcendence abolished, a state of things that is given and does not have to be surpassed. But then, what shall we do there? In order for the air there to be breathable, it must leave room for actions and desires; we must have to surpass it in its turn; it must not be a paradise. The beauty of the promised land is that it promised new promises. Immobile paradises promise us nothing but an eternal ennui. Pyrrhus speaks of resting only because he lacks imagination. Once returned home, he will hunt, he will legislate, he will go to war again. If he tries to stay truly at rest, he will only yawn. Literature has often described the disappointment of the man who has just attained the ardently desired goal: and after that? One cannot fulfill a man; he is not a vessel that docilely allows itself to be filled up. His condition is to surpass everything given. Once attained, his plenitude falls into the past, leaving that 'constant emptiness of the future' [*creux toujours futur*] of which Valéry speaks gaping open. Such are the passionate lovers described by Marcel Arland or Jacques Chardonne. They wish to settle down forever at the heart of their love, and soon, enclosed in their solitary retreat, without having stopped loving each other, they get desperately bored. 'Happiness is nothing more than this then!' says the heroine of *Terres étrangères* [Foreign Lands]. Each object, each instant, reduced to its immediate presence, is not enough for a man. He is himself not enough for himself since he is always infinitely more than he would be if he were only that. To live a love is to throw oneself through that love toward new goals: a home, a job, a common future. Since man is project, his happiness, like his pleasures, can only be projects. The man who has made a fortune immediately dreams of making another. Pascal said it perfectly: it is not the hare that interests the hunter, it's the hunt. One is wrong to reproach a man for struggling for a paradise in which he would not wish to live. The goal is a goal only at the end of the path. As soon as it is attained, it becomes a new starting point. The socialist wants the advent of the socialist State, but if that State were given to him at the outset, he would desire something else. From within the State, he would invent other goals. A goal is always the meaning and the result of an effort. Separated from that effort, no reality is a goal but only a given, made to be surpassed. This does not mean that only the struggle counts, that the stakes do not matter, as is sometimes said, because the struggle is a struggle for the stakes. If the stakes are taken away from it, the struggle loses all meaning and all truth. It is no longer a struggle but a stupid marching in place [*piétinement*].

The serious mind claims to separate the end from the project that defines it and to recognize in it an intrinsic value. He believes that values are in the world, before man, without him. Man would only have to pick them. But Spinoza, and Hegel, more definitively, have already dissipated this illusion of false objectivity. There is a false subjectivity that, in a symmetrical movement, claims to separate the project from the end and to reduce it to a simple game, a diversion. It denies that any value exists in the world because it denies man's transcendence and wants to reduce him to his immanence alone. A man who desires and who lucidly starts an undertaking is sincere in his desires. He wants an end; he wants it at the exclusion of any other end, but he does not want it in order to stop there, to enjoy it. He wants it in order for it to be surpassed. The notion of end is ambiguous since every end is a point of departure at the same time. But this does not prevent it from being seen as an end. Man's freedom resides in this power.

This very ambiguity seems to authorize the irony of the humorist. Isn't Pyrrhus absurd to leave in order to return home? Isn't the tennis player absurd to hit a ball in order for someone to send it back to him and the skier absurd to climb a slope in order to immediately come back down? Not only does the goal conceal itself, but the successive goals contradict each other, and the undertaking is completed only in destroying itself.

But here the humorist uses a sophism. He decomposes all human activity into elementary acts whose juxtaposition appears contradictory. If he completed the decomposition to recover the pure instant, then all contradiction would disappear. Only a shapeless incoherence would remain, a pure contingency that would neither outrage [*scandaliser*] nor astonish. But he is cheating. He maintains the existence of partial meanings that oppose each other at the heart of the ensemble whose global meaning he rejects. One says that the skier only climbs up in order to come down. Then one is admitting that he climbs, that he comes down, that his movements do not follow each other randomly but aim for the top of the hill or the bottom of the valley. One therefore grants the existence of synthetic significations toward which every element transcends itself. But it is then a purely arbitrary decision to reject the idea of a greater ensemble where the ascent and the descent surpass themselves toward a walk or an exercise. It is not up to the humorist to decide; it is up to the skier. Pyrrhus would be absurd if he left in order to return home, but it is the humorist who introduces this finality here. He does not have the right to extend Pyrrhus's project farther than Pyrrhus has settled upon. Pyrrhus is not leaving in order to return; he is leaving in order to conquer. That undertaking is not contradictory.

A project is exactly what it decides to be. It has the meaning that it gives itself. One cannot define it from the outside. It is not contradictory; it is possible and coherent as soon as it exists, and it exists as soon as a man makes it exist.

In this way, wisdom for man does not consist of withdrawing into oneself. The wise man himself who advises the immobility of rest to his disciples contradicts this advice by giving it; he should not say anything. He should not find himself disciples. Epicurus preaches ataraxia, but he preaches, and he preaches that it is necessary to preach; he preaches friendship. Neither does the Stoic remain stiffly in an indifferent freedom resting uselessly upon itself. He teaches all men the power of their freedom. And even when the wise man avoids loudly proclaiming the value of silence, he never succeeds in maintaining himself at the heart of himself and maintaining the world around him in an equal indifference. It doesn't matter to him whether he eats or fasts, governs an empire or lives in a barrel, but he still must choose: he eats or fasts, he rules or abdicates. Here lies the disappointing character of every conversion. I judge the movement of my transcendence to be futile [*vain*], but I cannot prevent it. Time continues to flow by; the instants push me forward. So I am wise, and what will I do now? I live, even if I judge that life is absurd, like Achilles always catching up with the tortoise despite Zeno.

Each man decides on the place he occupies in the world, but he must occupy one. He can never withdraw from it. The wise man is a man among men, and his very wisdom is a project of himself.

Infinity

Why then would Candide choose to assign no limit to his garden? If man is always somewhere else, then why isn't he everywhere? Expanded to the borders of the world, would he experience that rest he was looking for by contracting into himself? If I am everywhere, where will I go? Movement disappears here as surely as if I were nowhere. 'That little boy was not your brother,' said the parents to their oversensitive son. They added, 'You are not going to cry your whole life. Each day there are thousands of children across the earth who die.' Not all our life, so why five minutes? Not over all children; why over this one? If all men are my brothers, no particular man is my brother any longer. Multiplying the ties that bind me to the world by infinity is a way of denying those that unite me to this singular minute, to this singular corner of the earth. I no longer have a homeland, nor friends, nor parents. All figures disappear; they are reduced to the universal ground whose presence cannot be distinguished from absolute absence. Here also, there is no longer desire, nor fear, nor hardship, nor joy. Nothing is mine. Eternity joins with the instant; it's the same naked facticity, the same empty interiority. It is undoubtedly not by chance if the psychasthenic who denies himself the world and who renounces his transcendence is so often haunted by the idea of the impersonal infinity of this world. A needle, a subway ticket makes him dream about all needles, about all subway tickets in the world, and, stunned by this dizzying multiplicity, he remains immobile, using neither his needle nor his ticket.

Stoicism shows us how these two paths join together. If the wise man reduces himself to a pure upspringing of being falling back upon himself, he merges with the universal harmony at the same time. Destiny can have no hold on me since there is no longer anything that is outside of me. My own self is abolished within the universal. Spread out to infinity, my place in the world is erased just as if I had succeeded in containing it in one dimensionless point.

But this effort to identify myself with the universal immediately receives a denial. It is impossible for me to assert that it is the universal, that is, since I am asserting it. By asserting, I make myself be; it is I who am. As I distinguish myself from my pure presence by reaching out toward something other than me, I also distinguish myself from this other toward which I reach by the very fact that I reach toward it. My presence is. It breaks up the unity and the continuity of that mass of indifference into which I wanted it to be absorbed. Spinoza's existence sharply contradicts the truth of Spinozism. Hegel declares in vain that individuality is only a moment of the universal becoming. If this moment, as unsurpassed, had no reality, then it should not even exist in appearance; it should not even be named. If there is a question about it, the question gives it a truth that asserts itself against any surpassing. Whatever the truth of the sun and of man in the heart of the all, the appearance of the sun for man exists in an irreducible manner. Man cannot escape his own presence or that of the singular world that his presence reveals around him. His very effort to tear himself away from the earth only carves out his place there. Spinozism defines Spinoza, and Hegelianism defines Hegel. Flaubert believes he has rejoined the universal when he writes in substance: 'Why concern myself with the proletariat of today rather than the slaves of antiquity?' But by saying so he escapes neither his era nor his class. On the contrary, he behaves like a nineteenth-century bourgeois whose fortune, pastimes, and vanity mask his solidarity with his time.

Man can neither indefinitely reduce his being, nor expand it to infinity. He cannot find rest, and yet what is this movement that leads him nowhere? One finds the same antinomy in the realm of action as in that of speculation. Any stopping is impossible because transcendence is a perpetual surpassing. But an indefinite project is absurd since it leads to nothing. Here man dreams of an ideal symmetrical to that of the unconditioned God called for by speculative thought. He demands an unconditioned end for his acts such that it could not be surpassed, a term at once infinite and complete in which his transcendence would grasp itself anew without limiting itself. He cannot identify himself with infinity. But within his singular situation can he destine himself to it?

God

'God wills it.' This saying sheltered the Crusaders from the questions of Cineas. The conquests of the Christian warriors were not a vain pursuit, like those of Pyrrhus, if they were willed by God. One does not surpass the will of God. Man meets an absolute end of his efforts in God because there is nothing outside of him. The necessity of the divine being extends over those actions that end with him and saves them for eternity. But what does God will?

If God is infinity and the plenitude of being, there is in him no distance between his project and his reality. What he wills is; he wills what is. His will is only the immobile foundation of being; one can barely still call it a will. Such a God is not a singular person. He is the universal, the unchangeable and eternal everything. And the universal is silence. He demands nothing; he promises nothing; he requires no sacrifice; he dispenses no punishment or reward; he can justify nothing, nor condemn anything. One can found neither optimism nor despair on him. He is; one can say nothing more. The perfection of his being leaves no place for man. To transcend oneself in an object is to found it, but how can one found what already *is?* Man cannot transcend himself in God if God is completely given. Man is then nothing but an indifferent accident on the surface of being. He is on earth like the explorer lost in a desert. He can go to the right, to the left; he can go where he wants, but he will never go anywhere, and the sand will cover up his tracks. If he wants to give meaning to his behaviour, he should not address himself to this impersonal, indifferent, and complete God. His motto would be the one proposed on the pediment of the abbey of Thélème: 'Do what thou wilt.' If God wills all that is, man has only to act however he wants. 'When one is in God's hands, one need not worry about what one has to do; one has no remorse about what one has done,' said the heretical sect of Amalricians in the twelfth century. And they squandered their lives in joyous orgies.

The Church burned the Amalricians with great pomp. There exists, however, a Catholic naturalism that extends the benediction of God over the entire earth. We find an echo of this, for example, in Claudel. Everything comes from God, therefore everything is good. Man does not have to turn away from the earth, and he even has a lot of trouble corrupting this original destination within him because he is a creature of God. It is difficult to do evil because what is, is the good. But an orthodox Christian avoids taking such a thought to the extreme. 'Well, dear ma'am,' says the worldly and gourmand priest as he sits down at the table, 'Would God have invented all these good things if he did not want us to eat them?' But he is carefully forgetting that God also invented woman. There was an old woman who, outraged, refused to put butter in her soft-boiled egg. 'I eat it like the dear Lord made it,' she said. And she reached for the salt shaker.

'We shall pray to God with his entire oeuvre! Nothing that he does is in vain; nothing is foreign to our salvation!' cries Claudel. If God's oeuvre is completely good, it is because it is completely useful to the salvation of man. It is therefore not an end in itself, but a means that gets its justification from how we use it. But then how do we know if the melon was really invented to be eaten with our family? Maybe it was invented to not be eaten; maybe the goods of this world are good only because man can refuse them. This is why Saint Francis of Assisi smiled at the world but did not partake of it. 'For all things, you have but praise,' says the archaeologist to the viceroy of Naples, in the *Soulier de satin* [The Satin Slipper] [1929] by Claudel. 'But it angers me to see that you use none of it.' However, the viceroy gives away the riches that he does not use, and to give something away is a way of using it. Asceticism is another form of pleasure. Whatever he does, man makes use of earthly goods because through them he accomplishes his redemption or his ruin. He must therefore decide how to make use of them. His decision is not written in the object because any use is surpassing, and the surpassing is not given anywhere. It is not; it has to be [*a à être*]. What does it have to be?

It has to be in accordance with the will of God, says the Christian.

So one renounces all naturalism. Nothing is good

except virtue; evil is sin, and virtue is the submission to divine exigencies. There are, therefore, exigencies in God. He waits for man to destine himself to him. He created man so that there exists a being who is not a given but who accomplishes his being according to his creator's desire. The will of God then seems like an appeal to man's freedom; it demands something that has to be, that is not yet. It is thus project; it is the transcendence of a being who has to be its being, who is not. So a relationship between God and man is conceivable. As long as God is not all that he has to be, man can found him; he finds his place in the world. He is in situation with respect to God. And this is how God seems to be in situation with respect to man. This is what the German mystic Angelus Silésius means when he writes, 'God needs me as I need him.' The Christian then finds himself in front of a personal and living God *for* whom he can act. But in this case, God is no longer the absolute, the universal. He is that false infinity about which Hegel speaks who allows the finite facing him to subsist as separate from him. He is for man a neighbour.

This definite, singular God could satisfy the aspirations of human transcendence. He would indeed be a concrete being, complete and closed in upon himself, because he would exist and at the same time be indefinitely open because his existence would be an endless transcendence. He could not be surpassed, because he would himself be a perpetual surpassing. Man could only accompany his transcendence without ever transcending it. When I have accomplished the will of God, a new will will grab me; there will never be any 'after that?'.

But the will of this God is no longer written in things, because it is no longer the will of what is, but of what has to be. It is no longer the will of everything, and man must discover its singular shape. To want the will of God: this entirely formal decision is not sufficient to dictate any actions to man. Does God want the believer to massacre the unfaithful, burn the heretics, or tolerate their faith? Does he want him to go off to war or to make peace? Does he want capitalism or socialism? What is the temporal and human side of the eternal will? Man claims to transcend himself in God, but he never transcends himself except in the heart of immanence. He must accomplish his redemption on earth. Which of the earthly undertakings will raise him up to heaven?

'Let us listen to the voice of God,' says the believer. 'He will tell us himself what he expects of us.' But such a hope is naïve. God could manifest himself only through an earthly voice because our ears can hear no other. But how, then, does one recognize its divine nature? Upon asking a hallucinating woman who that interlocutor was who spoke to her by mysterious waves, she responded cautiously, 'He says that he is God, but I don't know him.' Moses could have felt the same mistrust about the voice that came out of the burning bush or that rumbled at the top of Mount Sinai. Whether the voice comes from a cloud, a church, or a confessor's mouth, the transcendent must always manifest himself through an immanent presence in the world. His transcendence will always escape us. Even in my heart, this order I hear is ambiguous. There lies the source of Abraham's anguish, which Kierkegaard describes in *Fear and Trembling* [1843]. Who knows if it's not a question of a temptation of the devil or my pride? Is it really God who is speaking? Who will distinguish the saint from the heretic? Kafka describes the same uncertainty in *The Castle* [1926]. Man can receive messages and even see the messenger. But isn't this one an impostor? And does *he* know who sends him? Hasn't he forgotten half the message along the way? Is this letter that he hands over to me authentic, and what is its meaning? The Messiah says that he is the Messiah; the false messiah also says it. Who will distinguish one from the other?

One will be able to recognize them only by their

works. But how will we decide whether these works are good or bad? We will decide in the name of a human good. All morality that claims to justify itself by divine transcendence proceeds this way. It posits a human good and affirms that it is willed by God because it is the good. Claudel asserts that we must prefer order to disorder because order is, while disorder is the negation of being; because order is in itself superior to disorder we proclaim that it conforms to God's designs. But Claudel is forgetting that, as Spinoza and Bergson have shown, only man's point of view makes order seem like order. Is Claudel's order the same as God's? There is a bourgeois order, a socialist order, a democratic order, a fascist order, and each one is disorder in the eyes of its adversary. Every society always claims to have God with it. It recreates him in its image; the society speaks, not God. But if I turn toward myself to question myself, I hear only the voice of my own heart. The Catholic Church and the Protestant individualist can rightly reproach each other for taking the echo of their personal convictions as a divine inspiration. I will not meet God himself outside of myself anymore than within myself. I will never notice any celestial sign written on the earth. If it is written down, it is earthly. Man cannot enlighten himself through God; through man one tries to shed light upon God. God's call [*appel*] is always made to be heard through men, and through human undertakings man will respond to this call [*appel*]. God, if he existed, would therefore be powerless to guide human transcendence. Man is never in situation except before men, and this presence or this absence way up in heaven does not concern him.

Humanity

We must therefore turn toward men. Can't we find in humanity itself that absolute end that we were first looking for in heaven? If we see it as closed upon itself, as needing to attain a state of unchanging equilibrium someday or to annihilate itself in death, we can undoubtedly transcend it toward nothingness and anxiously ask ourselves: and after that? If, with Laforgue, we imagine the terrestrial globe rolling frozen through a silent ether, what good does it do to preoccupy ourselves with the transient fauna that lives on it? But those are the visions of poets, wise men, or priests. Nothing allows us to affirm that humanity will ever die out. We know that each man is mortal but not that humanity must die. And if it does not die, it will never stop in any stage; it will not cease to be a perpetual surpassing of itself. However, if we envision only the indefinite nature of this race where one generation follows another only to disappear in turn, then it seems to us rather useless [*vain*] to take part in it. Our transcendence would be dissipated in time's elusive flight. But humanity is more than this endless dispersion; it is made of flesh-and-blood men. It has a singular history, a definite shape. In order for us to be able to transcend ourselves safely toward humanity, it must present itself to us in these two aspects at once: as open and as closed. It must be separated from its being so that it has to realize its being through us, and yet it must be. This is how humanity appears to those who propose the cult of Humanity to us. It is never completed; it unceasingly projects itself toward the future. It is a perpetual surpassing of itself; an appeal in need of a response constantly emanates from it; a void in need of fulfillment is constantly being hollowed out in it. Through each man, humanity searches indefinitely to rejoin its being, and its very being consists of that. Our transcendence can never surpass humanity but only accompany it, and yet it will be completely grasped again in each instant because in each instant Humanity is.

But *is* it really? Can one speak of *a* humanity? Undoubtedly it is always possible to use a collective noun for the ensemble of men, but this would be to consider them from the outside, as objects unified by the space that they take up. This collectivity would be only a herd of intelligent animals. We have nothing to do with this given, fixed in the plenitude of its being. In order for us to be able to act *for* humanity, it must demand something from us. It must possess a unity acting as a totality that seeks to realize itself, and it must appeal to us in a single voice.

Humanity takes this form in the myth of solidarity. Often since the famous apologue of the limbs and the stomach, men have been represented as the parts of an organism. By working for one of them, one would be working for them all. There is said to exist a natural economy according to which the place of each one is defined by the place of all the others. But this is defining man in terms of exteriority. In order to occupy a determined [*déterminée*] place in the world, man himself must be determined: a pure passivity. He would not, then, put the goal of his actions into question; he would not act. But he does act; he does question himself. He is free, and his freedom is interiority. How, then, would he *have* a place on earth? He will *take* a place by throwing himself into the world, by making himself exist among other men through his own project. Often the young man agonizes: how to integrate oneself into this plenitude? No drop of water is lacking from the sea. Before his birth, humanity was exactly as full; it will remain as full if he dies. He can neither diminish nor increase it, any more than a point can increase the length of a line. He does not feel at all like a cog in a precise mechanism. On the contrary, it seems to him that no corner of the world was reserved for him: he is everywhere too much [*de trop*]. And indeed, his place was not marked ahead of time as an absence. He came first. Absence does not precede presence; being precedes nothingness, and only through man's freedom do voids and lacks spring up in the heart of being.

It is true that at every moment men make this void spring up around them. In transcending the given toward a plenitude to come, they define the present as a lack. They constantly wait for something new: new goods, new techniques, social reforms, new men. And the young man encounters even more precise appeals around him; each year a certain number of government workers, doctors, fitters are needed; the world *lacks* manpower. He can slip into one of these voids, but there is never one that is moulded exactly for him. He can become one of those new men for whom others were waiting, but the new man they awaited was not *him*. Another would have done just as well. The place that each one occupies is always a foreign place. The bread that one eats is always the bread of another.

And besides, if I wait for men to give me a place, I would not know where to put myself; they do not agree with each other. The country lacks men; it makes that decision for itself. In the eyes of the neighbouring country, it is overpopulated. Society needs government workers to persevere in its routines, but the revolution needs militants who undermine society. A man finds his place on earth only by becoming a given object for other men, and every given is destined to be transcended. One transcends it by using it or combating it. I am an instrument for some only by becoming an obstacle for others. It is impossible to serve them all.

Wars, unemployment, crises plainly show that there doesn't exist any pre-established harmony between men. Initially, men do not depend on one another because initially they *are* not: they have to be. Freedoms are neither unified nor opposed but separated. In projecting himself into the world, a man situates himself by situating other men around him. So solidarities are created, but a man cannot enter into solidarity with all the others, because they do not all choose the same goals since their choices are free. If I serve the proletariat, I combat capitalism; the soldier only defends his country by killing its adversaries. Class and country define themselves as a unity through the unity of their opposition to the other. There is a proletariat only as long as there is a struggle against capitalism. A country exists only through its borders. If one does away with opposition, the totality comes apart; we are no longer dealing with anything but a plurality of separate individuals. In transcending oneself toward the proletariat, one cannot at the same time transcend oneself toward all of humanity because the only way to transcend oneself toward the proletariat is to transcend oneself with it against the rest of humanity. One might say that with the proletariat, one transcends oneself toward a future humanity where the separation of the classes will be abolished, but one must first expropriate one or several generations of capitalists and sacrifice the proletarians of today. One will always work for certain men against others.

Nevertheless, can't one count on a higher reconciliation beyond these oppositions? Don't singular sacrifices find a necessary place in world history? The myth of evolution wants to delude us with this hope. It promises us the accomplishment of human unity across temporal dispersion. Here transcendence takes the shape of progress. In each man, in each of his actions, the entire human past is written and immediately surpassed entirely toward the future. Reflecting upon old technologies, the inventor invents a new technology, and pushing off from this springboard, the following generation invents a better technology. The innovator salutes the success of his own project in this future humanity who only surpasses it by pushing off from it. 'Those who are born after us will, because of us, belong to a history higher than any other one ever was until us,' writes Nietzsche in *The Gay Science*. In this way human transcendence would be entirely grasped again within each moment because within each moment the preceding one would be conserved. And yet it would not become fixed in any of them, since progress always continues.

But the idea of evolution assumes a human continuity. In order for an action to persist in time like waves in ether, humanity must be a docile, passive medium. But how is it, then, that man acts?

If my son is a determined [*déterminé*] being who submits to my actions without resistance, then I am also determined; I do not act. And if I am free, my son is also free. But then my action cannot be transmitted across successive generations as if it were gliding along calm water. Other men act on this action in turn. Humanity is a discontinuous succession of free men who are irretrievably isolated by their subjectivity.

So an action thrown into the world is not

propagated infinitely like the wave in classical physics. Rather, the image proposed by the new wave
mechanics would be appropriate here: an experiment can define a wave in terms of probability and
give an equation for its propagation, but it does not
allow us to predict a later experiment that will
throw new givens into the world from which the
wave must be reconstructed anew. The action does
not stop the instant that we accomplish it. It escapes
us toward the future, where it is immediately
grasped again by foreign consciousnesses. It is never
a blind constraint for the other but a given to be
surpassed, and the other surpasses it, not I. From
this fixed act, the other throws himself into a future
that I have not mapped out for him. My action is
for the other only what he himself makes of it. How
then would I know in advance what I do? And if I
don't know, how can I intend to act for humanity? I
build a house for the men of tomorrow; perhaps
they will shelter themselves there, but it could also
get in the way of their future constructions. Maybe
they will put up with it; maybe they will demolish
it; maybe they will live in it, and it will collapse upon
them. If I bring a child into the world, tomorrow he
might be a criminal, a tyrant. He is the one to decide,
and each of his children's children will decide for
himself. Do I then procreate for humanity? How

many times has man exclaimed, 'I didn't want that to happen!' when contemplating the unexpected result of his action. Nobel thought he was working for science; he was working for war. Epicurus did not anticipate what would later be called Epicureanism, nor Nietzsche Nietzscheanism, nor Christ the Inquisition. Everything that comes from the hands of man is immediately taken away by the ebb and flow of history, remoulded by each new minute, and gives rise around it to a thousand unexpected eddies.

There are nevertheless some goals upon which human freedoms agree. If I intend to enlighten humanity, to increase its power over nature, to improve its hygiene, isn't the destiny of my action certain? The scholar is content if he brings a tiny rock to the edifice of science; it will remain eternally in its necessary place, and eternity will infinitely increase its dimensions.

It is true that men agree about science, since a thought is scientific only when it is such that all men can agree upon it. But in working for science, is it really for humanity that one works? Each one of its inventions defines a new situation for men. To decide that it is useful, the situation that it creates must be better than the former situation. Generally, the idea of progress requires such comparisons. But can one compare the diversity of human situations? Whether there are fifty million men on earth or twenty, humanity is exactly as full, and in its heart, it still has that 'constant emptiness of the future' that prevents it from ever becoming a paradise. If it can be seen as a goal impossible to surpass, it is because humanity itself is not limited to any goal. By its own *élan* it sets goals that constantly draw back before it. But this is when what seems to us to be the promise of salvation turns against our hopes: neither science, nor technology, nor any sort of action will ever bring humanity close to this moving goal. Whatever situation is created, it is, in its turn, a given to be surpassed. A successful man is said to have 'arrived'. Where has he arrived? One never arrives anywhere. There are only points of departure. With each man humanity makes a fresh start. And that's why the young man who seeks his place in the world does not initially find it and feels forsaken, useless, without justification. Whether he studies science, writes poetry, or builds motors, he transcends himself; he transcends the given situation, but he does not transcend himself for humanity. Humanity transcends itself through him. This transcendence isn't *for* anything; it is. Each man's life and all of humanity thus appear absolutely gratuitous at every instant, as neither required nor called [*appelées*] by anything. Their movement creates requirements and appeals to which only the creation of new requirements will respond. No accomplishment is merely imaginable.

But can this endless becoming itself be considered an accomplishment? Humanity does not move closer to a goal that has been fixed from the start, but if in each one of its successive stages the preceding one is conserved and takes on a higher form, couldn't we speak of progress? We see a contradiction in it, Hegel tells us, only because we stop at some of its avatars. But if we envision the totality of its history, we see the apparent separation of events and men vanish; all moments are reconciled. The obstacle is part of the struggle that breaks through it; cubism combats impressionism, but the former exists only through the latter, and the painting of tomorrow will be defined by going beyond them both. Robespierre is brought down by the revolution of Thermidor, but Robespierre and Thermidor together are found in Bonaparte. By realizing his historic and singular destiny, each man can thus find his place at the heart of the universal. My accomplished act becomes something other than what I had first wanted it to be, but it does not undergo a foreign perversion because of this. It completes its being, and thus it truly accomplishes itself.

In order to subscribe to Hegelian optimism, it must be established that the synthesis effectively

conserves the thesis and the antithesis that it surpasses; each man must be able to recognize himself
in the universal that envelops him. He must recognize himself there, says Hegel, since the concrete
universal is singular, and it is through singular indi-
vidualities that it finds its shape. It would not be
what it is if each of its moments had not been what
it was. Let us therefore admit that the presence of
each man is written in the world for eternity. Would
a defeated man be consoled by showing him that the
triumph of his victor would have been less brilliant
without his resistance? Would that be sufficient to
make that victory his own? To tell the truth, it is *his*
defeat that belongs to him. We have seen that man
is present in the world in two ways: he is an object,
a given that foreign transcendences surpass, and he
is himself a transcendence who throws himself
toward the future. What is his is what he founds by
his free project, and not what is founded by others
based on him. But what is conserved of a man in the
Hegelian dialectic is precisely his facticity. The truth
of a choice is the living subjectivity that makes it a
choice of that end, and not the fixed fact of having
chosen. Hegel retains only this dead aspect. As long
as he falls into the world as a thing passed by and
surpassed, man cannot find himself there. On the
contrary, he is alienated there. One cannot save a

man by showing him that that dimension of his being by which he is a stranger to himself and an object for others is conserved. Undoubtedly man is present to the entire universe as a given. At each instant, I have the entire past of humanity behind me, before me its entire future; I am situated in one spot on the earth, in the solar system, among the nebulae. Each of the objects that I handle refers me to all the objects that constitute the world, and my existence refers me to that of all men, but this is not sufficient for the universe to be mine. What is mine is what I have founded; it is the accomplishment of my own project.

And also, Hegel would say, man will indeed find the accomplishment of his project in universal becoming, if only he knew how to extend that project far enough. The only disappointment will be for the foolish stubbornness that will persist within a finite purpose. But if man adopts the universal's point of view, he will recognize his victory even in the appearance of defeat. Demosthenes was short-sighted when he was in despair over the ruin of Athens; what really mattered to him was civilization, and it was civilization that Philip and Alexander realized in the world. All is well if only I am capable of wanting it all.

But is such a desire possible?

Sheltered in the unique and impassive heaven, the wise man would see revolutions pass by like shadows on the eternally changing face of the earth. He would not lift a finger to secure the triumph of a certain shape of the world, which will be erased tomorrow. He would prefer nothing since all would be his. In this way the optimistic economist of the nineteenth century admires overpopulation for bringing an excess of labour and a correlative decrease in salaries, which leads to the mortality and sterility of the working class, thus leading back to depopulation, and so forth.

And indeed, if we are floating in Hegelian ether, neither the life nor the death of these particular men seems important to us. But why does the economic equilibrium still remain important? The universal spirit does not rejoice here over this machinery; the bourgeois economist does. The universal spirit is voiceless, and every man who claims to speak in its name only lends it his own voice. How could he adopt the universal's point of view since he is not the universal? One cannot have a point of view other than his own. 'Where is hell?' Marlowe's Faust asks Mephistopheles, and the demon replies, 'It is where we are.' Thus man can say, 'The earth is where I am.' There is no way for him to escape to Sirius. To claim that a man renounces the singular nature of his project is to kill the project. What Demosthenes really wanted was *one* civilization resting upon that of Athens, blossoming out of it.

Undoubtedly, it can happen that the project aimed for an end through means that have been shown to be inadequate. In this case, a man can congratulate himself on the success of another means that he had not initially chosen. A man desires the prosperity of his town; he votes for a leader. His rival is elected, but he shows himself to be a good leader; the town is prosperous in his hands. The voter can be satisfied with his election because the end for which he had aimed is accomplished in spite of everything. And it was a definite, singular end.

If one claims that every end can be seen as a means toward an end that is farther off, one denies that anything is really an end. The project is emptied of all its contents, and the world crumbles by losing all form. Man finds himself plunged into the heart of an expanse of equal indifference where things are what they are, without him ever choosing to make them be. Since there will always be a civilization, it may be useless to defend Athens. But then one must give up ever regretting anything or rejoicing for anything. To act for a goal is always to choose, to define. If the singular form of his effort appears to man as indifferent, his transcendence vanishes by losing all shape. He can no longer want anything since the universal is without lack, without expectation, and without appeal.

In this way, every effort by man to establish a relationship with infinity is futile [*vain*]. He can enter into a relationship with God only through humanity, and in humanity, he never reaches but a few men and can found only limited situations. If he dreams of expanding himself to infinity, he immediately loses himself. He loses himself in a dream because, in fact, he doesn't stop being there [*être là*], attesting to his finite presence by his finite projects.

Situation

Therefore, Candide's garden can be neither reduced to an atom nor merged with the universe. Man is only by choosing himself; if he refuses to choose, he annihilates himself. The paradox of the human condition is that every end can be surpassed, and yet, the project defines the end as an end. In order to surpass an end, it must first have been projected as something that is not to be surpassed. Man has no other way of existing. It is Pyrrhus, and not Cineas, who is right. Pyrrhus leaves in order to conquer; let him conquer, then. 'After that?' After that, he'll see.

Man's finiteness is therefore not endured [*subie*]; it is desired. Here, death does not have that importance with which it has often been endowed. It is not because man dies that he is finite. Our transcendence is always concretely defined on this side of death, or beyond it. Pyrrhus does not wait to have travelled around the world to return home; the revolutionary worries little about no longer being there the day that the revolution triumphs. The limit of our undertaking is at its very heart, not outside of it. A man takes a trip; he hurries to arrive in Lyon that evening because he wants to be in Valence tomorrow in order to be in Montelimar the day after tomorrow, in Avignon the day after that, in Arles the following day. One may laugh at him; whatever he does, he must return home without having seen Nimes, Marseilles; he won't have seen Rome or Constantinople. But that matters little to him; he will have taken the projected trip: his trip. The writer is impatient to have finished a book in order to write another one. Then I can die happy, he says, *my* work will be completed. He does not wait for death in order to stop, but if his project engages him right into future centuries, death will not stop him either. The octogenarian builds and plants; Moses knows that he will not enter into the Promised Land; Stendhal writes to be read a hundred years later. My death stops my life only once I am dead, and in the eyes of others. But for the living me, my death is not; my project crosses it without meeting obstacles. There exists no barrier against which my transcendence collides at full *élan*. It dies of itself, like the sea that runs into a smooth beach and comes to a stop and goes no farther.

Therefore, one must not say, with Heidegger, that man's authentic project is being for death [*être pour mourir*], that death is our essential end, that there is no other choice for man than the flight from or the assumption of this ultimate possibility. According to Heidegger himself, there is no interiority for men; his subjectivity is revealed only through an engagement in the objective world. There is choice only through an action that bites onto things. What man chooses is what he makes; what he projects is what he founds, but he does not make his death; he does not found it. He *is* mortal. And Heidegger has no right to say that this being is precisely *for* death. The fact of being is gratuitous; one is *for nothing*, or rather, the word *for* makes no sense here. Being is project because it posits an end, says Heidegger. But as being, being posits no end; it is. The project alone is what defines its being as being *for*. Heidegger agrees that, compared to other ends, this supreme end is not defined as an end by any act. The resolute decision that throws man toward his death does not lead him to kill himself, but only to live in the *presence of* death. But what is presence? It is nowhere else than in the act that presences [*présentifier*]; it is realized only in the creation of concrete links. Thus the Heideggerian conversion is shown to be as ineffective as the Stoic conversion. After, as before, life continues, identical. It is only a matter of an interior change. The same behaviours that are inauthentic when they appear as flights become authentic if they take place in the face of death. But this phrase *in the face of* is only a phrase. In any case, while I am living, death is not *here*, and in whose eyes is my behaviour a flight if for me it is a free choice of an end? Heidegger's hesitations concerning the degree of reality of inauthentic existence have their source in this sophism. In truth, only the subject defines the meaning of his action. There is no flight except through a project of flight. When I love, when I desire, I flee nothing: I love; I desire. The nothingness that anguish reveals to me is not the nothingness of my death. It is the negativity at the heart of my life that allows me to constantly transcend all transcendence. And the consciousness of this power is translated not by the assumption of my death, but rather by this 'irony' of which Kierkegaard or Nietzsche speaks: even though I would be immortal, even though I would try to identify myself with immortal humanity, every end would remain a departure, every surpassing an object to surpass, and that in this game of relationships there is no other absolute than the totality of these very relationships, emerging in the void, without support.

Thus one is not *for* death [*pour mourir*]; one is, without reason, without end. But as J.-P. Sartre has shown in *L'être et le néant* [Being and Nothingness] [1943] man's being is not the fixed being of things. Man has to be his being. Every moment he is seeking to make himself be, and that is the project. The human being exists in the form of projects that are not projects toward death [*projets vers la mort*] but projects toward singular ends. He hunts, he fishes, he fashions instruments, he writes books: these are not diversions or flights but a movement toward being; man makes so as to be [*faire pour être*]. He must transcend himself since he is not, but his transcendence must also grasp itself anew as a plenitude since he wants to be. Within the finite object that he founds, man will find a fixed reflection of his transcendence. Why will he found this object rather than that one? One cannot respond to this question because, precisely, the project is free. An existential analysis would allow us to extract the global meaning from a man's different choices, and to understand its development and its unity. But it would have to come to a halt before the uncompromising fact of that singular option by which each man freely throws *himself* into the world. We do not want to examine the contents of the project here, but, its original and free character being posited, we are only trying to define the general and formal conditions of its existence.

We have arrived at the conclusion that the project is singular and therefore finite. The temporal dimension of transcendence is not desired for itself; it depends on the nature of the founded object. A man may want to construct an edifice that will last through the centuries; he may also endeavour to succeed in a dangerous leap. He does not aim here at time for itself; time is only one particular quality of the object. In any case, whether it passes in an instant or endures across centuries, the object always has a duration [*durée*]. The plenitude of being is eternity. The object that will collapse one day is not, truly. 'And after that?' Man seeks to grasp his being again, but he can always transcend anew the object in which his transcendence is engaged. Even were it indestructible, the object would appear only as contingent, finite, a simple given that must still be surpassed. The object is sufficient as long as it is sufficient to me, but reflection is one of the forms that transcendence spontaneously takes on, and, in the eyes of reflection, the object is there, without reason. A man alone in the world would be paralyzed by the manifest vision of the vanity of all his goals. He would undoubtedly not be able to stand living.

But man is not alone in the world.

PART 2

Others

'How lucky she is!' said a psychasthenic watching a woman who was crying. 'She is crying *for real*.' The psychasthenic also cried rather often, but they weren't real tears; *her* tears were a comedy, a parody. The normal man does not think he is made of glass or wood. He does not think he is a puppet or a ghost, yet neither can he ever fully believe in his tears or his laughter. Nothing that happens to him is completely true. However long I look at myself in a mirror and tell myself my own history, I never grasp myself as a solid object. I feel within me that void which is myself; I feel that I *am* not. And that is why any cult of the self is truly impossible; I cannot destine myself to myself. Often in my youth I was in despair over not having any personality while certain classmates dazzled me with the brightness of their originality. The other easily takes on that marvellous and inaccessible character because he alone experiences for himself the void in his heart. For me, he is an object in the world, a plenitude. I who am nothing, I believe in his being, and yet he is also something other than an object. He has the infinity of his transcendence that can constantly push back the horizon toward which it rushes. I don't know if God exists, and no experience can make him present for me. Humanity never realizes itself. But the other is there, before me, closed upon himself, open onto infinity. If I destined my actions to him, wouldn't they also take on an infinite dimension?

As soon as a child has finished a drawing or a page of writing, he runs to show them to his parents. He needs their approval as much as candy or toys; the drawing requires an eye that looks at it. These disorganized lines must become a boat or a horse for someone. So the miracle is accomplished, and the child proudly contemplates the multicoloured paper. From then on there is a real boat, a real horse there. By himself, he would not have dared to put confidence in those hesitant lines. Undoubtedly, we do not try to thus change all the instants of our lives into hard diamonds. We often seek to accomplish our being without help; I walk in the country, I break off a stem, I kick a pebble, I climb a hill; all that without witnesses. But no one is satisfied with such solitude for his entire life. As soon as my walk is completed, I feel the need to tell a friend about it. King Candaule wanted his wife's beauty to shine for everyone's eyes. Thoreau lived for years in the woods, alone, but upon returning he wrote *Walden* [1854]. And Alain Gerbault wrote *Seul á travers l'Atlantique* [The Flight of the 'Firecrest']. Even Saint Teresa wrote *The Interior Castle*, and Saint John of the Cross his canticles.

What, then, do we expect from others?

I would be wrong to hope that others could take me far away across an endless becoming. No human act is propagated to infinity; what others create based on me is no longer mine. The sick person whom I cure may be hit by a bus his first time out; I do not say that my care killed him. I bring a child into the world; if he becomes a criminal, I am not an evildoer. If I claimed to assume for infinity the consequences of my actions, I could no longer want anything. I am finite; I must desire my finitude. But what I desire is to choose an end that could not be surpassed, that would truly be an end. And if the object, fixed upon itself, is not sufficient to stop me, wouldn't others have this power?

Devotion

Let's suppose the other needed me and that his existence had an absolute value. Then my being is justified since I am for a being whose existence is justified. I am released from both the risk and the anguish. By positing an absolute end before me, I have abdicated my freedom; questions are no longer posed; I no longer want to be anything but a response to that appeal which requires me. The master is hungry and thirsty; the devoted slave desires only to be the dish that he prepares and the glass of water that he brings to appease the hunger and thirst; he makes himself into a docile instrument. If his master requires it, he will kill himself, and will even kill his master because there exists nothing beyond the master's will, not even what might seem to be his own good. To attain his being, the slave wants to be a thing before the one who possesses being. Many men, and even more women, wish for such a rest: let us devote ourselves.

But first, to whom shall I devote myself? The value of the life to which my own is destined must appear as absolute to me. If a woman asked herself what her old, incompetent husband was good for, she would also ask herself: what's the use of devoting myself to him? She avoids asking herself questions, but then her security is rather precarious because the question may be asked at any moment. I will tranquilly devote myself only if I will the existence of the other in an unconditioned way. Such a will may spring up out of love, admiration, or respect for the human person. Is it then legitimate to dedicate myself, body and soul, to this child, master, or invalid? Will my being be able to accomplish itself in this way?

The devoted man often complains of meeting with only ingratitude around him; his kindnesses go unnoticed or even seem irritating. The justification that he was expecting is refused him by the very person who alone could grant it to him. He bitterly invokes man's perversity. But aren't there more specific reasons for this ingratitude? Does devotion ever conform to what it claims to be? And does it ever attain the results that it intends?

'I did not ask to be born,' says the ungrateful child. These words sting his father to the quick because devotion appears first of all as a total resignation [*demission*] in favour of the other. 'I lived only for you; I sacrificed everything for you,' says the father. But he must clearly recognize that he couldn't resign in favour of what did not yet exist. To bring a child into the world is not to devote oneself to anyone. It is indeed to throw oneself into the world by way of an anonymous child, without submitting to any foreign will. 'So be it,' says the father, 'but ever since the child was born, he has asked for and demanded things, and I gave him what he wanted.'

'If he gave me everything, it's because he wanted to,' says the ungrateful child, and indeed, the father gave in freely to his demands. A man can never abdicate his freedom; his claims to renounce it are only a masquerade that he freely performs. The slave who obeys chooses to obey, and his choice must be renewed at every moment. One is devoted because one wants to be; one wants to be because one hopes to regain his being in this way . . . 'I gave you my life, my youth, my time,' says the scorned woman. But what would she have done with her youth and her time if she had not given them away? In love and friendship, the word 'gift' has a rather ambiguous meaning. The adulated tyrant thinks that he is doing his slave a great favour by accepting his services. He would be right if the slave were content with his slavery. The mother who contemplates her grown son like the volunteer nurse who contemplates her cured patient, says with regret, 'You no longer need me!' This regret often takes on the form of a reproach. The need that I saw in the other was therefore really a gift that he was giving me. It is hard to say who are the winners and losers. The object of devotion very often feels irritation; he asked for nothing. His mother, his wife, or his friend ask that their devotion be accepted. They rejoice in the other's misfortunes because they hope to console him and they feel betrayed and blame him when happiness renders them useless. Far from being a resignation, devotion very often takes on an aggressive and tyrannical shape. We want the other's good without him and against him.

But is it indeed the other's good that one wants? It is evident that one can speak of devotion only on this condition. If I set a goal for myself that another did not set for himself, it is *my* goal, and I am not being devoted; I am doing. In looking at his son who did not ask to be born and who is presently a handsome and robust little boy, the father may proudly think: 'See what I have made,' and not 'See what I have devoted myself to.' There is devotion only if I take an end defined by the other as my end. But then it is contradictory to suppose that *I* could define that end for him. The despotic father who prevents his son from marrying whom he wishes would still like to think that he is devoted to him, but it is in the name of his own good that he chooses one situation rather than another for his son. He avoids taking responsibility for his own will by declaring that he acts for *the* good and posits the objectivity of accepted values such as health, fortune and glory. In Bernanos's *Journal d'un curé de campagne* [Diary of a Country Priest], the defrocked priest who bores his unfortunate companion stiff with his lessons believes he is acting for her own good. Isn't knowledge a good thing? Likewise the inquisitor has the heretic burned at the stake in the name of what is good; no one would claim that he is devoted to him. To devote oneself is to act *for* another, giving to the word 'for' the meaning of the German expression *warum willen* [*sic*]; it is to respond to the appeal that emanates from his will. His only good is what he wants as his good. When a man posits an end for itself unconditionally, then no one can deny it this character; and if he does not attain it, no foreign success could compensate for this failure. And, as Hegel has so clearly shown, we must ensure that the end includes the means by which we intend to reach it. Suppose a child tries to climb up a tree; a well-meaning and presumptuous adult lifts him off the ground and hoists him up to a branch. The child is disappointed; he wanted not only to be in the tree but to climb there himself. We see right away that there are certain goods that others cannot attain through us. We can do nothing *for* him unless he expects something from us, and by giving him precisely what he expects.

Many so-called devotions thus contradict what they claim from the beginning. They are in truth tyrannies. But can there be devotions that are not tyrannical? Suppose I want to devote myself, knowing that in so doing I remain free, and that nothing will deliver me from the risk and anguish of my freedom. But if I freely choose to accept as my own end the end posited by the other's will, am I not really seeking his good?

But first I would have to know what the other's will is, and that is not so easy. Every project extends across time; it envelops a plurality of elementary projects. We must know how to distinguish those that accord with the essential project, those that contradict it, and those that relate to it only in a contingent manner. The other's will must be distinguished from his whims. Suppose the convalescent wants to go out despite the doctor's orders, and I give in to his wishes, causing him to become sick again. My excuse that 'I am not responsible; I did what he wanted,' would not be acceptable. 'You shouldn't have listened to me,' the patient himself will angrily say. After becoming a man, the spoiled child will address similar reproaches to his parents. They may seem harsh, but they are not unfair. Because I know the other's desires, I transcend them; they are only givens for me, and it's up to me to decide if they express his true will. For a man is something else besides what he is at this moment. No word, not even any gesture could define a good that surpasses each instant. It would be rather foolish to trust words: Orestes was careless in believing that Hermione wanted Pyrrhus's death because she demanded it at the top of her voice. Neither are singular behaviours sufficient to convince us; it is the totality of a life that we must be able to examine. Thwarting the ruses of bad faith, the psychiatrist discovers ends in his patient that are his own ends and yet which are completely different from those that the patient admits. We give credit to the lucidity of people whom we admire, whom we respect, but that again is a decision. The good of the other is what he wants, but when it is a matter of discerning his true will, we can only resort to our judgment alone.

Isn't that becoming a tyrant again? It would be easy for the despotic father to think that he judges what's good for his son better than his son does himself. 'Deep down,' he says, 'my son wants the same thing as I do. He persists out of ignorance, carelessness. He will recognize his error later on.' He appeals to his future son against his present son. But he will never be sure, in the future any more than in the present. Will the future submission be more real than today's revolt? If the latter does not worry the father, why would the docility on which he is counting satisfy him? It may even happen that some parents despair because they have been obeyed too well. They no longer recognize the voice of the little boy whom they have mastered in the mouth of the young man who accepts what they think is best for him. They did not want what's good for this young man, but what was good for the little boy as he would still exist in the young man. They were dupes, here, of an illusion. The successive moments of a life cannot be preserved in their surpassing; they are separated. For the individual as for humanity, time is not progress but division. Just as one can never act for humanity as a whole, one never acts for one entire man. A man's will does not remain the same during an entire life. Future blame or approval will not be an objective observation but a new project that enjoys no privilege over the project that it confirms or contradicts. There is no instant in a life where all instants are reconciled. Not only can one not know beyond doubt the other's good, but there is not *one* good that is definitively this good. One often has to choose between these different goods posited by a man's different projects. The child must be betrayed for the man, or the man for the child.

One therefore devotes oneself amid risk and doubt. We must take a stand and choose without anything dictating our choice for us. But posing such choices belongs precisely to our freedom. I choose to prefer the man to the child if it is the man whom the child will become, and not the child, who is of interest to me. Or I prefer the child because the child exists, and I love him, and I am indifferent to that future man whom I do not know. One cannot condemn devotion simply because it requires that our actions be limited to this or to that. We never act except by creating limits for ourselves.

Let's admit, then, that, conscious of the freedom of my actions, the risks that they involve, the limits of their success, I still decide to answer that appeal which wells up toward me. The child asks me for a toy; I give it to him; he is happy. Can't I be satisfied with his joy? The obliging mother looks at the child who is smiling at the toy and smiles, but her smile stiffens. Now the child wants a drum, a set of tools; the old toy no longer amuses him. 'After that?' he says impatiently. However hard his mother tries to satisfy him, there will always be an 'after that'. Devotion claims to fulfil the other, but one cannot fulfil a man. A man never arrives anywhere; one will wear oneself out by following him, without ever arriving either. Let us recall that man is transcendence; what he demands, he only demands in order to surpass. The sick man requires care; I give it to him; he recovers. But the health that he recovers through me is not a good if I stop him at that. It becomes a good thing only if he makes something of it. If I prevent him from using it, he will ask me angrily: 'Why have you saved my life? Why have you given it back to me?' This is why tales in which the hero, saved from mortal peril, is forced by his saviour to one preset day give up his own life for him seem so cruel to us. The saved man will give back something quite different from what he received, and the demanding benefactor looks like an unjust tyrant. I never create anything for the other except points of departure. The health, the instruction and the fortune that a father has provided for his son must appear not as givens to him, but as possibilities that only the son can use. I am not the one who founds the other; I am only the instrument upon which the other founds himself. He alone makes himself be by transcending my gifts.

The father and the benefactor often fail to recognize this truth. 'I am the one who made him what he is. I pulled him up from nothing,' they say about their obligee. They would like the other to recognize the foundation of his being in them, outside of himself. Such a gratitude is sometimes found. 'What would I have become without you?' says the distraught man snatched from a disaster. He refuses to project himself beyond that disaster; by saving his situation, one has saved *him*. But a proud man rebelliously refuses to be thus merged with a given thing, to deny his freedom. No matter what someone has done for him, he does not feel affected in his being. When it comes to his being, he is the only one who makes it. Therein lies the essential source of those misunderstandings that often separate the child from his parents: 'You owe your life to me,' says the father when demanding obedience from his son. But to give a life confers no right over a freedom. The father thinks that he has given his child the greatest of gifts since he brought him into the world, but the child knows that there is no world for him except through his presence in that world. He is himself only through his own project. His birth, his education are only the facticity that is for him to surpass. What one has done for him forms part of the situation that his freedom transcends. Though, of course, he had to be in one situation or another, he does not coincide with his situation since he is always elsewhere.

The fundamental error of devotion is that it considers the other as an object carrying an emptiness in its heart that would be possible to fill. Even when it aims at the future, it still assumes such a lack. A son wishes to marry; the marriage will impose heavy burdens upon him and risks leading him to misery. His father opposes it, saying: 'I am acting for his own good.' But how would he act for that man who does not yet exist and does not project before him any good? The father imagines his son as he would have been without him: an impoverished man, overwhelmed with worries. Then he imagines him as he will be thanks to him: rich and free; and he claims to see in the latter an impoverished man saved from misery by him. But the impoverished man does not exist anywhere; no appeal rose up from his lips; there was no emptiness there to fill. Likewise, a child who is happy to live is not a child who asked to be born and who was born. When I was little, I often thought with a sort of vertigo about all the children who would never be born, as if they had existed somewhere as a potentiality, as if they had been appeals not heard, voids not filled. But that was a childish imagination. Life is a plenitude preceded by no painful absence.

A Celtic legend recounts that someone predicted to a young woman that her child would be a 'worthy druid' if she brought him into the world that very night, and that he would be a great king if she didn't give birth until the next day. She heroically remained seated on a rock all night long, and the child wasn't born until the morning. He had a flattened head, but he was a great king. Obviously the heroic mother did not devote herself to her son. Insofar as he already existed, he was asking only to be born. And if one questions the future, one thinks that if he had been a wise druid, he would have been happy to be one. In choosing the existence of a king, one has rejected that of a druid. In either one, the child would have fully realized his destiny. In a way, a man is always all that he has to be, since, as Heidegger shows, it is his existence that defines his essence. However, one must not believe that the young mother acted for *herself*. The error of an ethics of self-interest is the same as that of devotion. One assumes that an emptiness was there first, in me or in another, and that I would not have been able to act if the place for my action had not already been carved out. But our actions are not waiting to be called forth [*appelées*]; they are rushing toward a future that is not prefigured anywhere. Our actions always create a future, and the future explodes into the full world like a new and gratuitous plenitude. One does not desire for others or for oneself; one desires *for nothing*, and that is what freedom is. It is for nothing that the young mother in the legend wanted a son who would be a king; for nothing that a flesh-and-blood mother wants her son to become a strong, rich, educated man. And that is exactly what makes for the touching character of maternal love, properly understood. We must know that we never create anything for the other except points of departure, and yet we must want them for ourselves as ends.

The generous man knows well that his action reaches only the outside of the other. All that he can ask is that this free action not be confused with a pure facticity without foundation, that it be recognized as free by the one who benefits from it. The ingrate often refuses such a gratitude. He does not like to admit to himself that he was viewed as an object by a foreign freedom; he only wants to believe in his freedom alone. So he tries his best to not think of his benefactor, or he claims to see only a mechanical force in him. He explains: the benefactor acted out of vanity, out of a sense of importance. If his decision appears to be subject to a psychological determinism, it is no longer offensive; it is no longer anything but a simple fact among others. In enlightened, consenting gratitude, one must be capable of maintaining face to face these two freedoms that seem to exclude each other: the other's freedom and mine. I must simultaneously grasp myself as object and as freedom and recognize my situation as founded by the other, while asserting my being beyond the situation.

It is not a matter of paying off a debt here. There exists no currency that allows for paying the other in return. Between what he has done for me and what I will do for him, there can be no measure. In order to get rid of all worries about gratitude, it happens that a man tries to reimburse a kindness with gifts. These gifts are not touching; they wound. They appear to be the price of a favour whose value one is therefore claiming to measure like that of a thing. A tip given in thanks for a generous act is insulting. It is a way of denying the act its freedom by supposing that it was not done freely, for nothing, but out of self-interest. Generosity wants and knows itself to be free and asks for nothing but to be recognized as such.

A lucid generosity is what should guide our actions. We will assume our own choices and posit as our ends the situations that will be new points of departure for others. But we must not delude ourselves with the hope that we can do anything *for* others. That is what we learn in the end from this analysis of devotion: its pretensions cannot be justified; the goal that it proposes to itself is impossible. Not only are we unable to abdicate our freedom in favour of the other, or ever act entirely for one man, but we cannot even do anything for any man. Since there exists for him no immobile happiness with which we can gratify him, no paradise into which we can make him enter, his veritable good is that freedom which belongs only to him and which brings him beyond every given. It is out of our reach. Even God would have no hold on it.

And if I can do nothing for a man, I can do nothing against him either. The disappointment of the mother who does not succeed in completely fulfilling her child corresponds to the exasperation of the executioner who is challenged by a proud soul. However hard he tries, if his victim wants to be free, she will remain free even during torture, and struggling and suffering will only elevate her. One can kill her only because she was carrying her death in her. From what point of view can we say that it is an evil that this death occurred today rather than tomorrow? How can one harm a man? Did it harm Socrates to make him drink the hemlock? Did it harm Dostoevsky to send him to the penal colony?

Of course, violence exists. A man is freedom and facticity at the same time. He is free, but not with that abstract freedom posited by the Stoics; he is free in situation. We must distinguish here, as Descartes suggests, his freedom from his power. His power is finite, and one can increase it or restrict it from the outside. One can throw a man in prison, get him out, cut off his arm, lend him wings, but his freedom remains infinite in all cases. The automobile and the airplane change nothing about our freedom, and the slave's chains change nothing about it either. He freely lets himself die or gathers his strength to live; he freely resigns himself or he revolts; he always surpasses himself. Violence can act only upon the facticity of man, upon his exterior. Even when it stops him in his *élan* toward his goal, violence does not reach him in his heart because he was still free in the face of the goal that he proposed to himself. He wanted to succeed without merging with his success. He can transcend his failure as he would have transcended his success. And that is also why a proud man refuses pity as he refused gratitude; he is never fulfilled, but he is never without resources. He does not want others to pity him. He is beyond his misfortune as he is his happiness.

We are therefore never anything but an instrument for the other, even when we are an obstacle, like the air that supports Kant's dove while resisting it. A man would be nothing if nothing happened to him, and it is always through others that something happens to him, starting with his birth. One cannot treat the other as an instrument if he refuses to be one. On the contrary, I am the instrument of his destiny. And this is why our actions toward the other seem to us so heavy and at the same time weightless. No doubt, the life of the other would have been completely different if I hadn't crossed his path, pronounced those words, if I hadn't been there. But that would have been *his* life; through him our words and our gestures received a meaning. He freely decided their meaning. Everything around him would have been as full if I had not existed.

Must we, then, conclude that our conduct toward the other does not matter?

Far from it. It is indifferent *for him*, because it is a part of those things that the Stoics would call 'ouk ephiemenon', things that we ourselves have not wanted. But it concerns me, it is my conduct, and I am responsible for it. The most striking illustration of this paradox is found in the Christian religion. The Christian is *for others* only an instrument in the hands of God, and yet he is accountable to God for all *his* actions. What good is it to care for the sick and relieve the suffering when sickness and misery are tests willed by God and good for the soul? In order to justify himself, a Christian father whose tyrannical conduct provoked or hastened the death of his daughter said, 'After all, I was only an instrument in the hands of God.' The Christian knows that through him it is always God who acts. Even if he leads his neighbour into temptation, it is because the neighbour was supposed to be tempted. And yet Christ said, 'Woe to those who cause others to sin.' The sincere and scrupulous Christian rejects this weak defence, 'I am but an instrument', because if he is only an excuse for others, an occasion for salvation or ruin, he is free before God. Death is not an evil for the man whom I kill; through my crime, God's will calls him home. And yet in killing him, I, myself, have sinned. A given for others, my act is a free act for me. And in this way, from the Christian point of view, it is never for others that one can want anything; it is for God. One must accomplish one's own salvation. One cannot bring about the other's salvation, and that is the only good that exists for him. This truth can be expressed in another language: as freedom, the other is radically separated from me; no connection can be created from me to this pure interiority upon which even God would have no hold, as Descartes has clearly shown. What concerns me is the other's situation, as something founded by me. One must not believe that I could elude the responsibility for that situation on the pretext that the other is free. That is his business, not mine. *I* am responsible for what I can do, for what I am doing. There is a convenient and false way of thinking that authorizes all abstentions, all tyrannies. Peaceful and satiated, the egoist declares, 'The unemployed, the prisoners, the sick are as free as I am; why reject wars or misery if a man remains just as free in the worst circumstances?' But only the impoverished man can declare himself free in the midst of his misery. In abstaining from helping him,

I am the very face of that misery. The freedom that rejects or accepts it absolutely does not exist for me. It exists only for the one in whom it is realized. It is not in his name; it is in the name of *my* freedom that I can accept or reject it.

And I must accept or reject. I say that I can do nothing for the other or against him, but that does not release me from caring about my relationship with him because whatever I do, I exist before him. I am there, and for him, I am confused with the outrageous [*scandaleuse*] existence of all that is not him. I am the facticity of his situation. The other is free based on that, totally free based only on that, but free facing this and not that, facing me. The fate that weighs on the other is always us. Fate is the fixed face that the freedom of all the others turns toward each of us. It is in this sense that Dostoevsky said that 'each person is guilty for everything, before everyone.' Immobile or in action, we always weigh upon the earth. Every refusal is a choice, every silence has a voice. Our very passivity is willed; in order to not choose, we still must choose not to choose. It is impossible to escape.

Communication

An initial analysis of my relationships with others has thus led me to this result: the other asks me for nothing and he is not a void that I would have to fill; I can discover no ready-made [*toute faite*] justification of myself in him. And yet each of my actions by falling into the world creates a new situation for him. I must assume these actions. I want certain situations and I reject others. But why is it, then, that they do not appear to me as indifferent, that I can choose between them? In what way do they concern me? What is my true relationship with the other?

We must first turn away from the errors of false objectivity. The serious mind considers health, fortune, education and comfort as indisputable goods whose worth is written in heaven. But he is duped by an illusion; ready-made values whose hierarchy is imposed upon my decisions do not exist without me. What's good for a man is what he wants as his own good. However, this will is not sufficient to define ours. Is it good that this man attains *his* own good? As we have seen, man himself is divided between his present and his future; we must often choose. And man is not alone in the world. What is good for different men differs. Working for some often means working against the others. One cannot stop at this tranquil solution: wanting *the* good of *all* men. We must define *our* own good. The error of Kantian ethics is to have claimed to make an abstraction of our own presence in the world.

Therefore, it leads only to abstract formulas. The respect of the human person in general cannot suffice to guide us because we are dealing with separate and opposed individuals. The human person is complete both in the victim and the executioner; should we let the victim perish or kill the executioner?

We have already seen that, if I efface myself from the world, if I have the contradictory pretension of judging human situations without adopting any human point of view on them, they appear to me as incomparable among themselves, and I can want nothing. An attitude of contemplation never allows any preference. It delivers what is with indifference. There is preference only when the subject transcends the object. One prefers for an end, from a definite point of view. One prefers one fruit over another in order to eat it or paint it, but if one had nothing to do with it, the word 'preference' loses all meaning. 'Do you prefer the ocean or the mountains?' It should be understood as: 'Do you prefer to live by the ocean or in the mountains?' If one doesn't care about sewing or riding a bicycle, one cannot choose between a bicycle and a sewing machine. A past moment can appear as better or worse to me to the extent that I transcend it with my own project. If I want the blossoming of culture, I prefer the Renaissance to the Middle Ages, and I consider it as a progression toward *my* end, but I can speak of progress only in relation to a goal that I have fixed. If I am transported outside of all situations, any given seems equally indifferent to me. So it is impossible for me to choose between the diverse moments of history; they appear as givens to me, identical in that they all represent the fixed *élan* of a transcendence, and radically heterogeneous in the singular facticity of their existence. One can establish a hierarchy neither in the heart of identity nor in absolute separation. Spinoza rightly said that one cannot compare the perfection of horses with that of dogs. How does one decide what is worth the most *in itself*: the life of a cathedral builder or that of a pilot? And if we consider the human essence that is common to them, it is complete in each one of them.

In *Histoire veritable* [True Story], Montesquieu tells that one day a genie offered a poor man his choice of becoming a king, a rich landowner, or an opulent merchant whose happiness he had so often envied. The poor man hesitated and in the end could not reconcile himself to any exchange; he remained himself. Each man is apt to envy the fate of another, Montesquieu concludes, but no one would accept to be the other. And in fact, I envy the situation of the other if it appears to me as a point of departure that I myself would surpass, but the other's being, closed upon itself, fixed and separated from me, can be made the object of no desire. It is from the core of my life that I desire, prefer and reject.

Answering the question 'How to choose?' is possible because each one of us is truly at the core of his life. 'I want the biggest piece,' says the child looking greedily at the cake that his mother has just cut up. 'Why would it be yours rather than another's?' 'Because it's me.' The clever businessman knows how to cultivate this taste for privilege in his clients: 'I'll let you have it for twenty francs, but only because it's you,' he says to the flattered housewife. She readily believes him. How could *I* be just anyone? Other men exist only as objects; we alone grasp ourselves in our intimacy and our freedom as a subject. What is puerile in the child and the housewife is believing that their privilege exists in the eyes of others, because each person is only a subject for himself. But it is true that I am just anyone only in the eyes of the others, and ethics cannot demand from me that I realize this foreign point of view. That would be to cease being me; it would be to cease being. I am; I am in situation before the other and before the situations in which he finds himself. And that is exactly why I can prefer and desire.

So we must now try to define what *my* situation

is before others. Only then can we attempt to find a foundation for our actions.

We have seen that it is only through the presence of man that what J.-P. Sartre calls *négatités*, i.e., voids, lacks, absences, seep into the world. Some men refuse to make use of this power. Everything around them is full; they see no place for anything else. Every novelty frightens them and reforms must be forcibly imposed upon them. 'One did fine in the past without these inventions,' they say. Others, on the contrary, are in a state of waiting; they hope and demand. But they never demand *me*, and yet I wish to be necessitated by them in the very singularity of my being. The book that I write does not fill a void shaped in advance exactly like it. The book is first, and once it is, it is up to the reader to grasp its presence as the reverse of an absence: his freedom alone decides. 'How could one do without railroads or airplanes? How can one imagine French literature without Racine or philosophy without Kant?' Beyond his present satisfaction, man retrospectively projects a need behind him. And indeed, now that it exists, the airplane responds to a need, but it is a need that it created by existing, or more exactly, that men freely created based on its existence. Human freedom must then carve out a place for this new plenitude that we cause to spring forth in the world.

This place was not, and neither are we the ones who made it; we have only made the object that fills it up. Only the other can create a need for what we give him; every appeal and every demand comes from his freedom. In order for the object that I founded to appear as a good, the other must make it into his own good, and then I would be justified for having created it. The other's freedom alone is capable of necessitating my being. My essential need is therefore to be faced with free men. My project loses all meaning not if my death is announced, but if the end of the world is announced to me. The time of scorn is also that of despair.

Thus it is not *for* others that each person transcends himself; one writes books and invents machines that were demanded nowhere. It is not *for* oneself [*soi*] either, because 'self' [*soi*] exists only through the very project that throws it into the world. The fact of transcendence precedes all ends and all justification, but as soon as we are thrown into the world, we immediately wish to escape from the contingence and the gratuitousness of pure presence. We need others in order for our existence to become founded and necessary.

It is not a matter of making recognized in us the pure abstract form of the self [*moi*], as Hegel believes. I intend to save my being in the world, such as it is realized in my actions, my works, my life. Only through these objects that I make exist in the world can I communicate with others. If I make nothing exist, there is neither communication nor justification. But many men fool themselves here. We have seen that, out of irresponsibility or laziness, man often claims to find his being where he has not engaged it and declares objects that he has not founded as his. He demands the other's approval for these foreign things, and he tries his best to believe that it's really *he* who benefits from it. In such a case a man is accused of stupid vanity, when, for example, he boasts about his ancestors, his fortune, or his good looks. In an even more puerile way, the jay adorns himself in peacock feathers and the handsome Christian borrows Cyrano's voice under Roxanne's balcony. But in the end, it is Cyrano whom Roxanne loves. If we really cared about ourselves, we would refuse to let ourselves be loved or admired for 'the wrong reasons', that is to say, through goods that are not our own. Thus some women want to be loved just as they are [*sans fard*], and some men, incognito. The conceited man seems to imagine that others possess being, and that one can capture this precious wealth by surprise, but others can only clothe with a necessary dimension what I do in order to make myself be; I must do something first. In this sense one is right to say that whoever seeks himself will lose himself, and that it is in losing himself that he finds himself. If I seek myself in the eyes of others before I have fashioned myself, I am nothing. I take on a shape and an existence only if I first throw myself into the world by loving, by doing.

And my being enters into communication with others only through those objects in which it is engaged. I must resign myself to never being entirely saved. There are endeavours that extend over an entire life; others are limited to an instant, but none expresses the totality of my being since this totality *is not*. We are often fooled by a mirage. If, for example, I have written two verses that are admired, I readily believe that I am necessitated, even in my way of eating and sleeping, because my self is dispersed and unified at the same time. It is like the mana of the primitive man – entirely whole in each point. And as the primitive man thinks that if one possesses a single hair of his, one possesses his entire mana, we imagine that the praise given to one of our actions justifies our entire being. This is why we worry about being named. The name is my total presence magically assembled into the object. But in truth, our actions are separate, and we exist for others only insofar as we are present in our actions, and therefore in our separation.

If first I must know *what* I communicate, it is no less important for me to know with whom I can and want to communicate. Looking for just any approval is another one of the weaknesses of vanity, as when Mr de Montherlant demands praise from critics whom he claims to scorn and asks for the admiration of a public that he judges to be imbecilic. Truly, in order for the other to possess this power of making the object that I founded necessary, I must not be able to transcend him in turn. As soon as the other appears to me as limited or finite, the place that he creates for me on earth is as contingent and useless [*value*] as himself. 'He needs me, but what need is there for him? How could this unjustifiable existence justify me?' The coquette looks at her suitor with disgust; if her beauty is useless in the depths of her mirror, isn't it also useless in the depths of his eyes? Many women give up their lovers on the advice of their concierges because the lover is only a man; the concierge is the voice of the public, that mysterious *they* that exists and yet extends to infinity. A writer looks up with satisfaction when someone tells him, '*They* admire you,' but as soon as he knows the name of his admirers, he is disappointed. Usually, the blame or the esteem of those close to us hardly touches us. We know their motives too well; they are facts that we can predict and transcend. Parents may be irritated to see their son give their lost prestige to a friend; the friend is a stranger whom the child does not transcend, while his parents have become fixed as objects in his eyes. In this way the man who suffers from an inferiority complex will not let himself be reassured by any approval. The one who approves of him is only a single individual; he transcends him toward that innumerable, mysterious stranger in whose eyes he feels inadequate. Inversely, a man can always believe himself to be an unappreciated genius. Those who condemn him are only finite individuals whose judgment he challenges in order to appeal to an enlightened, impartial, and free posterity.

For I must have a freedom facing me. Freedom is the only reality that I cannot transcend. How can one surpass what is constantly surpassing itself? If a being appears to me as pure freedom, if he is capable of founding himself entirely by himself, he can also justify what I have founded by taking it on as his own. Such a being would be God. The magic of love, fear, admiration and respect can change a man into God. The humble adorer is nothing but an object, and his idol is not an object before anyone; toward whom could one transcend this pure and sovereign freedom? There is nothing beyond it.

But if suddenly other freedoms are revealed to

me, the fascination dissipates. I remember the shock [*scandale*] I felt as a thirteen-year-old when a friend whom I admired violently contradicted an opinion of my father's. She judged my father; my father judged her in return. I could therefore appeal to my father against my friend, to my friend against my father. In this going back and forth, the absolute slipped away. I could no longer rely on anyone. My dismay lasted a long time. Whom should I care about pleasing?

I am dealing not with one freedom but with *several* freedoms. And precisely because they are free, they do not agree among themselves. Kantian ethics enjoins me to seek the support of all of humanity, but we have seen that there exists no heaven where the reconciliation of human judgments is accomplished. If certain works are hardly discussed anymore, it's because they have ceased to move us; they have become museum objects or relics. But one must not believe that they are justified simply because they are written down in history. Certainly without Sophocles or Malherbe, literature would not have been what it is, but that confers no necessity upon their works because literature need not be what it is. It is; that's all. Here, one finds the point of view of the universal that allows neither praise nor blame since no void within it could even be supposed. Success appears only through a definite project that posits an end and carves out a retrospective appeal behind it. The dilettante who claims to love everything loves nothing. In order to be pleased about the existence of Rimbaud or Cézanne, one must prefer a certain poetry and a certain way of painting above all others. An object is grasped as having needed to be what it has been only if a singular choice flows back from the future toward it. This very reality that we throw into the world will be saved only if others found a future that envelops it by surpassing it, and only if new objects choose it in the past for the future. We cannot, therefore, be satisfied with a simple verbal approval; only the conceited man is content with that because he is only looking for the hollow appearance of being. But a more demanding man knows that words cannot suffice to necessitate the object that he has founded. He asks that a real place be reserved for him on earth. It is not enough that others listen to my tale; the listener must wait hungrily for my words. A woman quickly tires of an indifferent admiration; she wants to be loved because love alone will create an essential need of her. The writer does not only want to be read; he wants to have influence, he wants to be imitated and pondered. The inventor asks that the tool he invented be used. But human projects are separate and may even fight against each other. To me, my being appears condemned to remain forever divided. A loyal ally is also a traitor, and a venerable wise man a corrupter. No man is a hero to his valet. I can laugh at the hero with the valet, but the hero and his friends will laugh at me. If I laugh at the valet, he will laugh at me at the same time as at the hero. However, if I laugh at everyone, I end up alone in the world and everyone will laugh at me.

The most convenient solution would be to challenge the judgments that bother me by considering the men who pass them as simple objects, denying them their freedom. 'They are barbarians, slaves,' thought the decadent Romans in seeing themselves cursed by the men working and suffering for them. 'He's a Negro,' thought the planter of Virginia. And by rigid taboos, these parasitic societies try their best to defend the masters against the consciousnesses of the creatures whom they are exploiting. They must not be recognized as men. It is told that some white women used to get undressed in front of Indo-Chinese servant boys with indifference; those yellow people were not men.

But then the parasite ignores the human character of the objects that he uses. He lives in the midst of a foreign nature, among inert things, crushed by the enormous weight of things and subjected to a mysterious fate. In the tools, the machines, the houses, and the bread he eats, he does not recognize the mark of any freedom. Only the matter remains, and to the extent that he depends on matter, he also is only matter and passivity. In suppressing man's empire over things, he makes himself a thing among things. And he gains nothing in this metamorphosis. If we assume that, for security reasons, one administered to the servants a magic potion that transforms them into beasts, no reconciliation would be thus realized between men. Faced with this new animal species, the masters would still constitute a divided humanity. The parasite becomes human again only in turning toward his peers, and he then finds himself in danger before their freedoms.

And besides, man is not free to treat other men as things, as he likes. In spite of taboos, prejudices and his wilful blindness, the master knows that he must speak to the slave. One speaks only to men. Language is an appeal to the other's freedom since the sign is only a sign through a consciousness that grasps it again. He feels the look of the slave. As soon as he is looked at, he is the one who is object. He is a tyrant who is cruel or timid, resolute or hesitant; if he tries to transcend that transcendence, thinking, 'Those are the thoughts of a slave,' he knows that the slave also transcends that thought, and in the struggle that unfolds here, the slave's freedom is recognized by the very defence that the master puts up. All men are free, and as soon as we deal with them, we experience their freedom. If we want to disregard these dangerous freedoms, we must turn away from men. But then our being draws back and loses itself. Our being realizes itself only by choosing to be in danger in the world, in danger before the foreign and divided freedoms that take hold of it.

However, we have a recourse against these freedoms: not stupid blindness but struggle, because we can in turn transcend the action by which they transcend us. 'Who will be my witness?' wonders the pilot in Saint-Exupéry's *Pilote de guerre* [Flight to Arras], who is sent on a dangerous mission at the moment of defeat. He challenges all testimonies; he himself witnesses others' cowardice and abandonment. I don't wish to be recognized by just anyone, because in communication with others, we look for the completion of the project in which our freedom is engaged, and therefore others must project me toward a future that I recognize as mine. For me it would be a bitter failure if my action were perpetuated by becoming useful to my adversaries. The project by which others confer necessity upon me must also be my project. There are blames and hatreds that I joyfully accept. The revolutionary who combats the conservative's project wishes to appear as a hostile force to him. In her memoirs, Gertrude Stein tells that Fernande Picasso was happy with a hat only if she heard bricklayers and workmen exclaim at length when they saw her, because for her, elegance was defined as a challenge to plain good sense. If we struggle against a project, we choose to appear as an obstacle before it. There are projects that simply do not concern us; we consider the judgments where they are expressed with indifference. If, for example, it is a question of appreciating a poem, a banker is not competent, and the banker would smile at the poet's advice. It may be that my disdain envelops not one particular competence but an entire man. It is the global project of his being that we reject and combat. So disdain becomes contempt. I am indifferent to any opinion of those whom I despise. 'I didn't ask you for your opinion,' one says in contempt, and even, 'I am not speaking to you.' For any speech, any expression is an appeal; true contempt is silence. It takes away even the taste for contradiction and for outrage. In the case of outrage, we ask that the other prove that his project is separate from ours. We want to become a ridiculous or hateful object for him. Thus there will no longer be complicity between us. But this is leaving him the initiative and consenting out of defiance to make ourselves into a thing. It is up to us to assert calmly that we are separating ourselves from him, that we are transcending him and that he is but an object before us.

It would be convenient to be able to use contempt as a weapon. One often tries hard to do this. A child or a young man, for example, who is esteemed by those around him chooses not to confront a foreign judgment face to face. He confines himself to his sphere and, in order to run no risk, disarms the rest of the world's opinion in advance. He goes through life with a sure step; whoever condemns him condemns themselves. But in doing this, he denies his freedom. To be free is to throw oneself into the world without weighing the consequences or stakes; it is to define any stake or any step oneself. The overly prudent man, on the contrary, must take care to not found any project other than that which enhances the prestige of the people who enhance his prestige. This timid vanity is the opposite of true pride. It also happens that a man who at first meets only with failure and disdain around him defends himself with repudiation. He wanted to be an athlete; he fails, so he begins to scorn athletes and sports. He esteems only bankers or soldiers now. But in thus renouncing his project, he betrays himself. And besides, one cannot at will cause contempt or esteem to be born within oneself. It is through the same project that, by defining the objects I found, I define myself and the public to whom my appeal is addressed. To love books, admire writers, and want to write: these were one and the same project for me in my childhood. Once the global choice has been posed we can partially contradict it only through blindness and bad faith, and bad faith carries doubt and uneasiness along with it. That is why so many conceited men are so unhappy with themselves. A fool always finds a greater fool who admires him, but he cannot at will hide from himself the fact that that fool is a fool, nor can he take foolishness for a virtue whenever it suits him. Freedom commands and does not obey. In vain does one try to deny or force it. If sports are truly my project, I still prefer being an unsuccessful athlete rather than being an honoured obese man. This is why one cannot so easily triumph, even interiorly, over a hated rival. If I want to be courageous, skilful and intelligent, I cannot scorn the courage, skill, or intelligence in the other.

The attitude of those who love only those who love them and indiscriminately scorn all those who scorn them is rightly seen as a weakness. One is rather suspicious that their love and their scorn are only a hollow appearance. Only by my free movement toward my being can I confirm in their being those from whom I expect a necessary foundation of my being. In order for men to be able to give me a place in the world, I must first make a world spring up around me where men have their place; I must love, want and do. My action itself must define the public to which I propose it. The architect loves to build; he builds an edifice that will remain standing for centuries; he appeals to a long posterity. An actor, a dancer appeal only to their contemporaries. If I perfect an airplane motor, my invention is of interest to millions of men. If it is a matter of getting approval for my daily actions or passing words, I address myself only to those who are close to me. I can concretely appeal only to the men who exist for me, and they exist for me only if I have created ties with them or if I have made them into my neighbours. They exist as allies or as enemies according to whether my project agrees with theirs or contradicts it. But how would I not assume this very contradiction since I am the one who makes it exist by making myself such as I make myself?

Action

So here is my situation facing others: men are free, and I am thrown into the world among these foreign

freedoms. I need them because once I have surpassed my own goals, my actions will fall back upon
themselves, inert and useless, if they have not been
carried off toward a new future by new projects.
A man who survives alone on earth after a world-
wide cataclysm must strive, like Ezekiel, to resuscitate
humanity, or he will have nothing left to do but die.
The movement of my transcendence appears futile
[*vain*] to me as soon as I have transcended it, but if,
through other men, my transcendence is always pro-
longed further than the project I am now forming,
I could never surpass it.

In order for my transcendence to be absolutely
impossible to transcend, all of humanity must
extend my project toward ends that were mine.
Who, then, would transcend it? Outside of it, there
would be no one, and it would be entirely my accom-
plice; no one would judge me. But I must renounce
this hope; men are separate, opposed. I must reconcile myself to the struggle.

But for *whom* shall I struggle? My goal is to
achieve being. Let's repeat again that it is not a question of egoism here. The idea of self-interest is based
on the idea of a ready-made self toward which the
subject that I am would transcend itself, taking it
for a supreme end, instead of throwing myself
through the project toward different ends of a self

that doesn't exist anywhere as a given. To seek to be is to seek *being*, because *there is no* being except through the presence of a subjectivity that discloses it, and it is necessarily from the heart of my subjectivity that I rush toward it. I therefore struggle in order to be. I struggle in order to possess a toy or a jewel, in order to take a trip, eat a fruit, or build a house. But that is not all. I adorn myself, I travel, and I build among men. I cannot live shut away in an ivory tower. Some theories such as those about art for art's sake are wrong to imagine that a poem or a painting is an inhuman and self-sufficient thing. It is an object made by man, for man. Of course, it is made neither to entertain nor to edify. It does not respond to a pre-existing need that it must fulfil. It is a surpassing of the past, a gratuitous and free invention, but in its newness, it demands to be understood and justified. Men must love it, want it, and prolong it. The artist cannot lose interest in the situation of the men around him. His own flesh is engaged in others. I will therefore struggle so that free men will give my actions and my works their necessary place.

But how does one resort to struggle here since these men must freely grant me their approval? Of course, wanting to obtain a spontaneous love or admiration by violence is absurd. One laughs at

Nero, who wanted to seduce by force. I want the other to recognize my actions as valid and to make them into his good by taking them up in his name toward the future. But I cannot count on such gratitude if I first contradict the other's project. He will see me only as an obstacle. I make an error in judgment if I force the other to live, even though he would like to die, on the pretext that I need a companion likely to justify my existence. He will curse me throughout his life. Respect for the other's freedom is not an abstract rule. It is the first condition of my successful effort. I can only appeal to the other's freedom, not constrain it. I can invent the most urgent appeals, try my best to charm it, but it will remain free to respond to those appeals or not, no matter what I do.

But in order for this rapport with the other to be established, two conditions must be met. First, I must be allowed to appeal. I will therefore struggle against those who want to stifle my voice, prevent me from expressing myself, and prevent me from being. To make myself exist before free men, I will often be compelled to treat some men as objects. A prisoner will kill his jailer to join up with his comrades. It's a shame that the jailer cannot also be a comrade, but it would be even more of a shame for the prisoner never to have any comrades again.

Next, I must have before me men who are free *for me*, who can respond to my appeal.

In any situation, the other's freedom is total because the situation is only to be surpassed, and freedom is equal in every surpassing. An ignorant man who strives to educate himself is as free as the scholar who invents a new hypothesis. We respect equally in all beings the free effort to transcend oneself toward being. What one scorns are the resignations of freedom. One cannot establish a moral hierarchy among human situations. But, as far as I am concerned, there are some of these transcendences that I can transcend, and that become fixed for me as objects. There are others that I can only accompany or that surpass me. Tess d'Urberville [*sic*] loves Angel Clare. The three farmer's daughters who also love Clare do not transcend Tess's love. With Tess, they transcend themselves toward Clare. But if we discover Clare's weaknesses, if we do not love him, all the while recognizing Tess's freedom, we see only an object that is foreign to us in her love. The other's freedom exists as separate from me only when it reaches for a goal that is foreign or has already been surpassed. The ignorant man who uses his freedom to surpass his state of ignorance can do nothing for the physicist who has just invented a complicated theory. The sick man who wears himself out by struggling against sickness or the slave against slavery care for neither poetry, nor astronomy, nor the improvement of aviation. They first need health, leisure, security and the freedom to do with themselves what they want. The other's freedom can do something for me only if my own goals can, in turn, serve as its point of departure. In using the tool that I have fabricated, the other prolongs its existence. The scholar can speak only to men who have arrived at a degree of knowledge equal to his own, so he proposes his theory to them as the basis for new work. The other can accompany my transcendence only if he is at the same spot on the path as I.

In order for our appeals not to be lost in the void, there must be men ready to hear me close by, and these men must be my peers. I, myself, cannot go backward, because the movement of my transcendence is carrying me ceaselessly forward, and I cannot walk toward the future alone. I would lose myself in a desert where none of my steps would matter. I must therefore strive to create for men situations such that they can accompany and surpass my transcendence. I need their freedom to be available to use and conserve me in surpassing me. I ask for health, knowledge, well-being and leisure for men so that their freedom is not consumed in fighting sickness, ignorance and misery.

Thus, man must be engaged in two convergent directions. He founds objects where he finds the fixed reflection of his transcendence. He transcends himself by a forward movement that is his freedom itself, and at each step, he strives to pull men to himself. He resembles the leader of an expedition who marks out a new route for his march and who constantly goes back to gather up the stragglers, running forward again to lead his escort further on. But, all men do not consent to follow. Some stay put or engage themselves on divergent roads. Some even try their best to stop his march and that of his followers. Wherever persuasion fails, only violence remains to defend oneself.

In one sense, violence is not an evil, since one can do nothing either for or against a man. To bring a child into the world is not to found him; to kill a man is not to destroy him. We never reach anything but the facticity of others. But precisely in choosing to act on that facticity, we give up taking the other for a freedom, and we restrict, accordingly, the possibilities of expanding our being. The man to whom I do violence is not my peer, and I need men to be my peers. The resort to violence arouses correspondingly less regret in cases where it seemed less possible to appeal to the freedom of the man to whom violence has been done. One unscrupulously uses force against a child or a sick person. But if I did violence to all men, I would be alone in the world, and lost. If I make a group of men into a herd of cattle, I reduce the human reign accordingly. And even if I oppress only one man, all of humanity appears in him as a pure thing to me. If a man is an ant that can be unscrupulously crushed, all men taken together are but an anthill. One cannot, therefore, lightheartedly accept resorting to force. It is the mark of a failure that nothing can offset. If the universal ethics of Kant and Hegel end in optimism, it is because in denying individuality, they also deny failure. But the individual is; failure is. If a scrupulous heart hesitates so long before making a political decision, it is not that political problems are difficult, but that they are unsolvable. And yet abstention is also impossible; one always acts. We are condemned to failure because we are condemned to violence. We are condemned to violence because man is divided and in conflict with himself, because men are separate and in conflict among themselves. Through violence the child will be made into a man and the horde into a society. Renouncing the struggle would be renouncing transcendence, renouncing being. However, no success will ever erase the absolute outrage of each singular failure.

We should not believe either that success consists of calmly attaining a goal. Our goals are never anything but new points of departure. Everything begins when we have led the other to this goal. From there, where will he go? I do not content myself with the idea that he will always go somewhere. Without me, he would have also been somewhere. I want it to be *my* project that he prolongs. It is up to each person to decide how far his project extends without being destroyed. Would Kant have found himself in Hegel? Would he have seen the Hegelian system as his negation? In order to respond, one must know what, in his eyes, the essential truth of his philosophy was. But in any case, his project did not extend to infinity. If Kant had wanted only philosophy, he would not have needed to write. In any event, philosophy existed. He wanted *a* philosophy created by a philosophical development that was his own. We want to be necessitated in our singularity, and we can be so only through singular projects. We depend on the other's freedom; he can forget, ignore, or use us for ends that are not our own. One of the meanings of *The Trial* [1925] described by Kafka is that no verdict can ever come to a conclusion. We live in a state of indefinite procrastination. This is also the meaning of what M. Blanchot says in *Aminadab:* the most important thing is to not lose, but one never wins. We must assume our actions in uncertainty and risk, and that is precisely the essence of freedom. Freedom is not decided with a view to a salvation that would be granted in advance. It signs no pact with the future. If it could be defined by the final point [*terme*] for which it aims, it would no longer be freedom. But an end is never a final point; it remains open to infinity. It is only an end because freedom stops there, thus defining my singular being at the heart of formless infinity. What concerns me is only to reach my end; the rest no longer depends on me. What the other will found based on me will belong to him and does not belong to me. I act only by assuming the risks of that future. They are the reverse of my finitude, and I am free in assuming my finitude.

Thus man can act; he must act. He is only in transcending himself. He acts in risk, in failure. He must assume the risk. By throwing himself toward the uncertain future, he founds his present with certainty. But failure cannot be assumed.

Conclusion

'And after that?' says Cineas.

I ask that freedoms turn back toward me in order to necessitate my actions. But can't reflection surpass this very action that claims to justify me? Men approve my work; their approval is in turn fixed as an object. It is as futile [*vaine*] as my work itself. Shouldn't one conclude that all is vanity?

What reflection reveals to me is that every project leaves room for a new question. Within myself I have a negative power with respect to my project and myself through which I appear as emerging in nothingness. It releases me from the illusion of false objectivity. I learn from it that there is no other end in the world besides my ends, and no other place besides the one that I carve out for myself. And other men do not have in their possession the values that I wish to attain either. If I transcend them, they can do nothing for me. In order to be recognized by them, I must first recognize them. Our freedoms support each other like the stones in an arch, but in an arch that no pillars support. Humanity is entirely suspended in a void that it creates itself by its reflection on its plenitude.

But since this void is only a reverse side, since reflection is possible only after spontaneous movement, why grant it a predominance and condemn human projects by comparing them with the tranquillity of nothingness? Reflection makes nothingness spring up around me, but reflection is not carried in its heart; it is not authorized to speak in its name and judge the human condition from its point of view. Wherever there is a point of view, there is not nothingness. And to tell the truth, I can take no other point of view but my own.

One and the same finite project throws me into this world and toward these men. If I love a man with an absolute love, his approval is sufficient for me. If I act for a city, a country, I appeal to my fellow citizens, to my fellow countrymen. If I create real ties between me and future centuries, my voice crosses the centuries. Of course, in any event, there is a point where my transcendence runs aground, but reflection cannot surpass it. I exist today, and today throws me into a future defined by my present project. Wherever the project stops, my future also stops, and if I claim to contemplate myself from the depths of this time where I am not, that is but a pretence and I am only uttering empty words. For eternity a minute is equal to a century, for infinity the atom is equal to the nebula. But I am floating neither in infinity nor in eternity; I am situated in a world that my presence defines. One only transcends oneself toward an end, and if I have precisely posited my end before me, toward what could I surpass it? Toward what could I transcend an exclusive love during the time that I love? When other men have begun to exist for me, then I could transcend that love. But I cannot transcend toward nothing the totality of men whom my project causes to exist for me.

One can surpass one project only by realizing another project. To transcend a transcendence is not to effectuate a progress, because these different projects are separate. The transcendent transcendence can in turn be transcended. No instant joins up with the eternal. Ecstasy and anguish still take their place in time; they are projects themselves. Every thought, every feeling is project. Thus the life of man does not appear as a progress but as a cycle. 'What good does it do?' he says, and he continues his task. I now see that moment of doubt or of ecstasy where all projects seem useless [*vain*] to me as a fit of ill humour or puerile exaltation. Between these two moments, who will judge? They exist together only by a third moment that must in turn be judged. That is no doubt why so much importance is attached to the last wish of a dying man. It is not only one wish among others, but it is the one in which the dying man has grasped his whole life again. Whoever wants to continue to affirm a dear friend's life against death prolongs his last instant by maintaining its privilege. It is only when I separate myself from the dead person in order to look at him from the outside that the last instant becomes an instant among others. Then the dead person is really dead; I transcend all his wishes equally.

We are free to transcend all transcendence. We can always escape toward an 'elsewhere', but this elsewhere is still somewhere, in the heart of our human condition. We never escape from that human condition, and we have no way to envision it from the outside in order to judge it. It alone makes language [*la parole*] possible. It is with our human condition that good and evil are defined. The words 'utility', 'progress', and 'fear' have meaning only in a world where the project has made points of view and ends appear. They presuppose this project and cannot be applied to it. Man knows nothing other than himself and cannot even dream of anything that is not human. To what can he therefore be compared? What man could judge man? In whose name would he speak?